CALLING AND CLARITY

CALLING AND CLARITY

Discovering What God Wants for Your Life

DOUG KOSKELA

WILLIAM B. EERDMANS PUBLISHING COMPANY

GRAND RAPIDS, MICHIGAN

Wm. B. Eerdmans Publishing Co.
2140 Oak Industrial Drive NE, Grand Rapids, Michigan 49505
www.eerdmans.com

26 25 24 23 22 21 20 19 18   3 4 5 6 7 8 9 10

Library of Congress Cataloging-in-Publication Data

Koskela, Douglas M., 1972-
Calling and clarity: discovering what God wants for your life / Doug Koskela.
pages   cm
ISBN 978-0-8028-7159-6 (pbk.: alk. paper)
1. Vocation — Christianity.
2. Discernment (Christian theology)   I. Title.

BV4740.K67   2015
248.4 — dc23

2014032510

2020-11

For Jamie

Contents

Acknowledgments

This book emerged from many conversations about vocation over the past thirteen years. Most of those conversations took place with students taking a first year seminar on "The Dynamics of Vocation" or a seminary course on "Vocational Discernment and Discipleship." Their keen insights and honest questions forged the categories at the heart of this discussion. I am very grateful for all that these students have contributed to my life and thinking, and I am glad that I have the opportunity to know and learn from them.

I wish to express my thanks to the Center for Scholarship and Faculty Development at Seattle Pacific University for a SERVE Grant that enabled me to complete the book. The director of the Center, Margaret Diddams, has supported this project in many ways over the last two years. I am also thankful for the various groups with whom I have been able to share and refine these ideas: attendees at the various Discernment Weekends at Seattle Pacific Seminary, members of the New Faculty Seminar at SPU, the Koinonia Class at First Free Methodist Church in Seattle, the Pastoral Staff at Timberlake Church, and the participants in the Business as a Calling Day in the SPU School of Business and Economics. Many thanks are also due to Mykylie Raymond-Myzak, my student assistant in 2012-13, who helped with many aspects of this project. I am also grateful to the many people at Eerdmans who made this a better book from start to finish.

In the pages that follow I reflect on the ways in which calling and response are reflections of God's grace. That is perhaps nowhere more evident than in parenting, and I give thanks daily for my son Nathan and my daughter Ally. Finally, words can't begin to express my appreciation for Jamie, my wife and best friend. It is a joy to share life with her, and to her this book is dedicated.

Introduction

A college student walked into her professor's office one afternoon. Her question was clear but daunting: "I want to serve God with my life, but I don't know where to begin. It's not clear to me what major would be best for me or in what career I can best serve God. How can I discern God's calling for my life?" Over the next hour, the professor invited the student into a conversation about what that process might look like. She asked what the student's passions were, what she was good at, and what genuine needs in the world she might be equipped to address. In the course of that conversation, it became clear to the student that the discernment process would take time and many more discussions such as this one. But the process had begun, and she became energized as she thought about the possibilities.

In Exodus 3, Moses walked beyond the wilderness to Horeb, the mountain of God. He wasn't seeking God's calling on his life; rather, he was tending his father-in-law's flock. Nonetheless, God gave Moses a very clear and direct calling: "I will send you to Pharaoh to bring my people, the Israelites, out of Egypt" (v. 10). Moses asked questions, claimed that he was not sufficiently eloquent for the task, and finally asked God to send someone else. His problem was not discerning his calling. His problem was responding faithfully to the calling that was clearly and directly placed upon him. Despite his hesitation and his sense of inadequacy, Moses was ultimately used by God to lead the Israelites out of Egypt.

These two stories about vocation — which is another word for calling — illustrate the problem that gives rise to this book. On the one hand, many of us can relate to the student in the first story. We desire to serve God with our lives, but we find it difficult to figure out just how. We may even desire a burning-bush experience that would clearly express God's plan for our lives. Yet even after much time and many anguished prayers, we often find that we still are not sure precisely what God wants for our lives. On the other hand, when we examine many of the famous call stories in Scripture, we find something very different. Like Moses, those in the Bible who are called to something often have very little doubt about what God wants them to do. Some examples would be the call stories of Jeremiah (Jeremiah 1), Jonah (Jonah 1), and Saul (Acts 9). Those who are called may hesitate to respond, and they may feel completely inadequate to the task. But their calling is clear and unmistakable. So we are faced with a disconnect between our own experience of seeking God's calling and many well-known call stories in Scripture. The disconnect can be expressed in terms of a series of vocational questions:

- Why am I not hearing anything from God when I'm trying so hard to discern God's will?
- Why do biblical characters such as Moses and Jonah receive a clear, unmistakable calling when they don't even appear to be seeking one?
- Why should I look to my gifts and passions to discern God's calling, when in Scripture God often calls people to tasks for which they are ill-equipped or don't want to do?

Much of the difficulty that arises when we begin to think about vocation is that the term itself can mean so many different things nowadays. For some of us, the first thing that enters our minds when we hear the word vocation is "career" — our vocation is how we make a living. Others might use the term "vocational training" to refer to acquiring particular job skills, often in contrast to a broader liberal arts education. In some contexts, having a vocation means that one is called specifically to the priesthood or to a religious order. (William C. Placher provides a helpful discussion of the various connotations of the word vocation in his introduction to *Callings: Twenty Centuries of Christian Wisdom on Vocation*.)

In what follows, though, we will be using the term more broadly than any of these options. At its heart, vocation refers to the various ways in which God calls us to live. We have choices to make about how we will use our time, our energy, and our gifts. The various levels of calling guide us in making good and faithful choices.

It has been common in the Christian tradition to think of two levels of vocation by drawing a distinction between *general calling* and *particular calling*. General calling refers to what God desires for all people, while particular calling refers to a task or purpose that God desires for a specific person. As we will see, this is a helpful and appropriate distinction to make. However, I want to suggest that it doesn't go far enough. There is another level of vocation that we will be wise to identify and keep in mind. Specifically, this book will argue that the category of particular calling really encompasses two very different sorts of calling: *missional calling* and *direct calling*. You will notice that the three categories of vocation that I am developing here are distinctive. For instance, they differ from the "three expressions of vocation" identified by Gordon T. Smith in his book *Courage and Calling*; in particular, his third category of "immediate call" differs substantially from what I am describing as direct calling.

The two stories above clearly illustrate my distinction between missional and direct calling. The college student in the first story was seeking to discern her *missional calling*, the specific guiding purpose God has given for her life that aligns with her gifts and passions. Moses, on the other hand, had received a *direct calling*, a clear calling from God to a particular task that a person may not be prepared for or want to do. A missional calling generally takes time, prayer, and the involvement of one's community to discern. The key questions are what God is calling us to and how we might live that calling out in particular situations. A direct calling, on the other hand, is generally apparent right away. The key question is whether we will be obedient to that calling. Once we are clear on the basic distinction between missional calling and direct calling, then we can make much better sense of both the biblical text and our own experience.

I would suggest that much of the frustration that people experience in trying to come to terms with their own calling arises from confusion about the different kinds of calling. In what follows, then, I aim to describe these three layers of calling in more detail. Chapter One will explore missional calling, which I believe is the primary focus of discernment during the young adult years. While some people come to recognize their missional calling earlier or later than that, one's undergraduate years are often filled with excitement and anxiety over the particular contribution that one might make to God's kingdom. Chapter Two will focus on the idea of direct calling. Even when a person senses God's clear guidance to perform a particular task or to set off on a particular journey, it can be difficult to listen. As in the case of Moses, the primary question with direct calling is not what God wants, but rather whether we will be obedient. We will also need to consider how we confirm that a supposed direct calling is really from God (rather than, say, our own desires). Chapter Three will consider the classic notion of general calling. Regardless of whether we have discerned our missional calling yet, and regardless of whether we have sensed a direct calling from God, our general calling can guide us in how we go about our day-to-day lives. We will come to see that there are many different ways in which Scripture describes our general calling — in fact, it would not be wrong for us to speak of general callings in the plural. Chapter Four will examine the process of vocational discernment, or how we come to know what God wants us to do with our lives. In particular, this chapter will focus on how we go about discerning our missional calling. Because the very idea of calling implies one who calls, Chapter Five will consider what all of this says about God. We will see the practical importance of such ideas as the Trinity, the relationship between God's action and human action, and worship as they apply to the idea of vocation.

While gaining clarity on the various kinds of calling is a good and important task, it is not the ultimate goal of the book. My ultimate aim is to help relieve some of the frustration that can arise as we seek to discern God's will, so that we may faithfully serve God with all of our lives. My hope is that we will cultivate hearts and minds that are attentive to God, seeking to understand our missional calling with the help of those who know us well. As we do so, our day-to-day choices can be shaped continually by keeping our general calling firmly in mind. Vocation, after all, is as much about how one treats one's roommate or co-worker as it is about the career one will pursue. And if we find ourselves clearly sensing a direct calling, leading us toward a task that we may not feel ready for, we will be well served if our lives are immersed in worship and the spiritual disciplines. Such practices cultivate the habit of obedience to God — a habit that will be crucial when God leads us out of our comfort zone. As we begin, then, let us always keep in mind that attentiveness and obedience to God are the heart of vocation.

What Is My Life About?
The Concept of Missional Calling

When Art was a child, his teachers often noticed his knack for creative thinking and his ability to express himself. ("Art" is a real person, and his story is used with permission, though his name has been changed.) Though he didn't particularly enjoy writing assignments early on, he received strong grades and encouragement from these teachers. He chose engineering as a major when he went to college, largely due to the advice from his uncle — an engineer himself — that the career outlook was very bright in that field. But just as he was realizing that he was miserable in his engineering classes, he also recognized that he enjoyed writing more and more. On top of that, he was still getting very positive feedback on his writing. In his junior year, Art finally decided to change his major to public relations with a minor in advertising. He also began to sense that he would like to use this ability in a very particular direction. He had enjoyed writing for the newsletter at his church, and he felt that he could help the church articulate its mission in promotional materials. This congregation eventually hired him onto its staff, and he found that he was able to live out what he enjoyed through his job.

Over the course of Art's career, his employment took many related shapes: he owned an advertising business for a time, and then he was hired as the marketing director for a music company.

Years later he took a job as sales director for a marketing firm. In all of these jobs, he was able to help congregations and Christian institutions articulate their unique vision to the public. Yet he found that he was also doing this in his spare time, writing freelance pieces for a Christian magazine. After he retired, he continued to do consulting work for congregations and volunteer work for his own church to help them convey their message. All the while, he was using his gifts to do something he enjoyed and ultimately, he hoped, to serve God.

A common thread through the various stages of Art's life was using his love for words and his ability for creative expression to help local congregations. This common thread is a good example of a *missional calling*. The term "missional calling" refers to the main contribution that your life makes to God's kingdom. You could think of it as the "mission statement" of your life. It refers to the distinctive direction in which you aim to spend the bulk of your time, gifts, and energy. To be sure, your contribution to God's kingdom is not limited to those things that fit neatly within your missional calling. Each person might be used by God in any number of ways, large and small. In Art's case, there were many ways in which he served God and people that did not connect to the common thread. But recognizing your missional calling is a way of acknowledging that God has wired you to serve in a particular, sustained way over a lifetime. Once you come to discern your missional calling, you often can see that you have already been working in that direction for some time. Furthermore, you begin to recognize fresh opportunities for that particular service in new and changing circumstances.

Grasping the idea of missional calling also helps you to avoid making two very common mistakes when thinking about vocation. The first mistake is to associate vocation exclusively with your job or career. While there is no doubt that a missional calling can be lived out significantly in a paid career, it is a much broader category than one's employment. The second mistake is to think of vocation only in terms of one particular situation or task. It might be tempting to think of "receiving a calling" only in terms of something like going to seminary or participating in a short-term mission to another country. While these examples represent one form of calling — direct calling, which Chapter Two will explore — they are not the only kinds of calling. As Art's story demonstrates, missional calling reflects a sustained and specific purpose that can find expression in many ways throughout your life.

Before I describe the concept in more detail, let me offer some more concrete examples. The possible examples of missional callings are practically limitless, but the following list gives a sense of the potential range:

- Improve life for children on the autism spectrum
- Make the gospel come alive in fresh ways for those who are already familiar with it
- Foster spiritual formation for young professionals
- Provide clean water to people who need it
- Help victims of abuse find restoration and healing

Features of Missional Calling

To get a clearer idea of missional calling, let's focus on five basic features. First, *missional calling generally aligns with your gifts*. The very idea of missional calling suggests that God has created each of you with certain abilities and gifts that should be used in God's service. It does not matter at this stage if you draw a distinction between natural talents and Spirit-endowed gifts. Even if such a distinction is drawn, both are ultimately from God. And to the degree that they are put to use in participating in God's creative and redemptive work, they are relevant to your missional calling. It must be said, of course, that you might well be called by God in some circumstances to tasks in which you are not particularly gifted. As Chapter Two will show, such was the case in many famous call stories in Scripture. But those instances are not what I mean by missional calling. Your missional calling is an ongoing pattern of using your gifts toward a particular purpose of significance to God's kingdom.

Second, *missional calling generally involves something you are passionate about and which gives you joy.* Over many years of talking to students about their sense of vocation, I have learned that many people are deeply afraid that God will call them to something they dread. And, to be honest, I cannot entirely promise that God will not do this — Jonah did not want to go to Nineveh, after all. But such instances, if and when they arise, are instances of direct calling rather than missional calling. They involve tasks to which God calls you for a very particular reason, whether you like what God is asking you to do or not. On the other hand, the sort of sustained, lifelong purpose expressed in a missional calling usually takes advantage of the unique passions that God has given to every one of you. Some of you take particular delight in working with children, while others find it very unnatural to do so. Some people find great joy in opportunities to speak before large groups of people, while that prospect is terrifying to others. As you listen for the shape of your particular missional calling, you would be wise to look to those things that you love. While you should always be obedient if you sense God clearly calling you to a specific task (even if it's something you don't want to do), your lifelong purpose usually goes with the grain of the passions that God has created in you.

A third feature of missional calling is that *it usually takes significant time, prayer, and communal involvement to discern.* While you might wish to run across a billboard that clearly and unmistakably tells you your life's purpose, it usually doesn't work that way. Instead, you will find that you need to spend considerable time praying, talking with those who love you and know you well, and paying attention to what you do well and what you enjoy. People often come to discover that their missional calling was present to some extent in their life even before they discovered it. For example, in his book *Let Your Life Speak*, Parker J. Palmer describes his childhood interest in airplanes. Not only did he enjoy crafting model airplanes, but he also spent countless hours carefully putting together books about aviation. As an adult reflecting back on this interest, he long supposed that he was inclined to be a pilot or an aeronautical engineer. But then he ran across some of these books in a cardboard box and discerned their vocational significance. He writes: "I didn't want to be a pilot or an aeronautical engineer or anything else related to aviation. I wanted to be an author, to make books — a task I have been attempting from the third grade to this very moment! From the beginning, our lives lay down clues to selfhood and vocation, though the clues may be hard to decode. But trying to interpret them is profoundly worthwhile" (p. 15). To be sure, Scripture indicates that there are times when God makes a calling very clear — but again, those instances are better categorized as examples of direct calling. When it comes to missional calling, the process can be considerably more messy and complicated. Chapter Four will explore in much more detail the process of vocational discernment.

Fourth, *missional calling is lived out in many ways throughout a person's life, not just through work.* Too often, people speak of trying to discern their calling when they really are thinking in terms of what their career should be. While it is certainly a good idea to think in terms of missional calling as you make choices about your career, you should recognize that missional calling is a broader category that is worth thinking about throughout your life. There are two very clear problems with associating missional calling only with your job. First, doing so presumes that you can fulfill your missional calling only at a stage of life when you are employed. But people who are in school, retired, or taking time away from a career for family reasons can still be living out their missional calling. Second, doing so presumes that you are living out your missional calling only during the hours you are at work. But a missional calling is something to which you can give much time and energy throughout the week. It might be expressed in time with family in the evening or in volunteer activities during the weekend. One of the marks of a missional calling is that it shows up in different ways in the various circumstances in your life. Sometimes consciously and sometimes below the surface, you will find that you tend to devote your time and energy to activities that connect in some way to this basic theme of your life.

A fifth dimension of missional calling is that, *generally speaking, people only have one such calling in their lifetime.* Of the five features I have identified, this one is likely to raise the most eyebrows. It is also the most flexible of the five features; it is not a hard-and-fast rule. It is true that people come to recognize gifts that they hadn't recognized before or find something that they truly love even late in life. It is also the case that some people experience dramatic transformations in their lives that reverse the course of their service to God. The last thing I would want to do is limit the ways in which God might work through a particular person. But identifying a singular missional calling does no such thing. People can and do make all sorts of contributions to God's kingdom that have no direct relationship to their particular missional calling. By suggesting that each person typically has only one such calling, I am trying to convey the nature of *this specific category* of calling. It is a way of saying that God has wired you in a particular way to make a unique contribution to God's purposes. Some people discover this relatively early in life, while others discover it much later. And it is not the case that this is the only contribution you will make — far from it. But if you look carefully at your life, you will discern a unique thread that runs through your gifts, your passions, and the various circumstances of your life. The sooner you recognize this thread, the more consciously and intentionally you will be able to find new ways of living it out. As you do, you will be working in concert with the distinct way that God has crafted you.

Missional Calling and Career

Having identified these features, let's consider the relationship between your missional calling and your career. It is clear that career and missional calling overlap for many people. While he doesn't use the category of missional calling, author and teacher Jerry Sittser offers a very helpful discussion of the distinction between career and calling in general in Chapter 12 of his book *The Will of God as a Way of Life*. In fact, daily work is one of the key means through which your missional calling can be expressed. When you think about serving God through your work, you might be inclined to think only in terms of things such as pastoral ministry or working with a Christian nonprofit organization. Or, extending a bit more broadly, you might think in terms of serving God in a particular profession such as education or medicine. Yet your missional calling can also involve all sorts of "everyday" work. Consider someone working for a catering business who finds a clear connection between her job and her missional calling to gather people together in fellowship around the table. Her professional training in culinary school, as well as the time she puts into promoting her business, hiring and supervising staff, and scheduling and billing each event all help her fulfill her missional calling of showing hospitality. Or imagine a stay-at-home father whose missional calling is to improve early childhood literacy. At other stages in his life, he might live this calling out in different ways — perhaps through political involvement, writing children's literature, volunteering as a tutor, developing software, or any other number of possibilities. But at this particular stage of his life, when his kids are very young, the work that consumes the majority of his time is to be a father. During those years that are filled with laundry, cooking, and bandaging wounds, he will also be able to live out his missional calling by helping his own kids learn to read and write.

Still, it is very important to remember that a career is not a missional calling itself. For example, suppose Carol discerns her missional calling to be helping senior citizens find and maintain housing. As an attorney, she might advocate for senior citizens on the brink of eviction or foreclosure as part of her work. Yet notice two things about this example. First, Carol will likely do all sorts of things as an attorney that do not directly relate to her missional calling. Indirectly, such work might be honing her legal skills to make her a more effective advocate, but there is no immediate relationship to her missional calling. I want to suggest that this is perfectly natural. In fact, the other work that her job requires may well have significant value in and of itself. You need not connect every aspect of your employment to your missional calling for both of them to be worthwhile. Second, Carol might live out her missional calling in many ways that do not involve her work as an attorney. Perhaps she volunteers on Saturday mornings for a Meals-on-Wheels program or donates money to a non-profit organization that helps senior citizens pay their heating bills. The point is that you should not force too close a connection between career and missional calling.

Pastoral ministry represents a unique case in the relationship between career and calling. Many pastors are paid a salary to minister in the context of the congregations they serve. At one level, then, pastoral ministry can be considered a career. (This is certainly not true for all pastors, of course, as many minister on a voluntary basis). At a deeper level, pastoral ministry is a calling. I would argue that a person should not go into pastoral ministry unless he or she has a confirmed calling from God to do so, and I suspect that most Christians would agree. However, I want to suggest that the call to pastoral ministry is *not* a case of missional calling — rather, it is a case of direct calling, which we will explore in Chapter Two. The direct, clear call from God to become a pastor, recognized by the church, is an essential requirement for those who will take that form of leadership in the church. Still, every pastor will find ways to live out his or her specific and unique missional calling in the course of pastoral ministry. In other words, every pastor has both a direct calling (to pastoral ministry itself) and a missional calling (the specific sense of purpose that gives shape to one's life and ministry). One pastor's missional calling might be holistic community development in an urban setting; another's might be extending Christ's love to socially marginalized youth; another's might be proclaiming the gospel to those who have seemingly given up on the church. In each of these cases, much of the work of pastoral ministry will not be directly connected to that specific missional calling. And in each of these cases, the missional calling will continue beyond a person's time as pastor in a particular setting (in retirement, for example).

A careful reader might have noticed something by now. Most of the examples thus far have involved professions that are options for those with a great deal of education and considerable social and historical advantages. But what about individuals — much of the world's population, really — who do not have access to those possibilities? What about those working on an assembly line, or laboring in an orchard, or scrubbing toilets? These questions help draw a distinction between employment and missional calling for two reasons. First, we should not uncritically associate God's will with the inequities and injustices of a fallen world. History is full of too many examples of arguments — usually offered by people in comfortable or advantageous situations — that some people must do back-breaking or tedious work precisely because God has called them there as their station in life. These arguments often serve more to ease guilty consciences than to tell us much about God's will. It is one thing to suggest that God can bring good in and through an economic system full of inequality and brokenness; it is quite another to suggest that the system itself is God's will.

Second, there is often significant meaning and value in such work, but not everything that gives meaning or has value represents a missional calling. For example, consider the employees who work long hours in a factory that makes infant car safety seats. There is inherent value in their work, as it helps to produce a good that saves lives. There is also instrumental value in their work, as it provides income for the employees and their families. Perhaps it also helps to cultivate virtues such as discipline, patience, and attentiveness. But none of this means that the missional calling of all of the employees is to make car safety seats for infants. Most of them, if not all of them, will have a very different missional calling that will be lived out through the various dimensions of their lives. The balance that I want to convey here is that there is potentially both inherent and instrumental value in all sorts of work, but your work does not determine the shape of your missional calling. If the topic of the inherent or "intrinsic" value of work in the context of the business world interests you, you can read more in Jeff Van Duzer's book, *Why Business Matters to God (and What Still Needs to Be Fixed)*.

Still, I think it would be a mistake to rule out the possibility that someone might partially live out a missional calling through work that is considered tedious or "unskilled." In the example of the car seat factory above, you could easily imagine someone working on the assembly line whose missional calling is to improve the well-being of babies. If so, you would not be surprised to see this missional calling also expressed in other ways in this person's life, such as volunteering weekends at a shelter for abused moms and their babies. (Of course, you could also imagine finding a similar missional calling in another employee of that company, such as the car seat quality control inspector or the company CEO.) Or, as another example, imagine someone whose missional calling is to create beauty in subtle, behind-the-scenes ways. Perhaps the bulk of his missional calling is lived out by creating works of art during his non-working hours. But he might also find another expression of that missional calling in his job as a night custodian in a grocery store, taking extra care to create a more inviting environment for employees and customers who spend time in the store. The main point here is that once a person discerns her missional calling, she will look wherever she can to find ways to live out that calling. Since most people spend a good portion of their adult lives in some sort of employment, it is good to find points of contact with your work whenever possible.

Missional Calling and the Kingdom of God

I have described missional calling as the unique and sustained contribution a person is called and equipped to make to the kingdom of God. Now I want to say a bit more about what is meant by the kingdom of God. For many of the examples so far relate to serving other people or improving life and well-being in particular contexts — is this really what is meant by contributing to the kingdom of God? Aren't these basically examples of service that are good and helpful but ultimately unrelated to God's eternal purposes? Isn't the kingdom of God about eternity in heaven rather than this world of mundane struggles and pursuits?

To begin to address these questions adequately, you need to recognize a couple of things. First, while I have tended to use the language of the kingdom of God in what I have said thus far, the Bible talks about the final result of God's redemptive work in a variety of other ways as well. Matthew's Gospel tends to talk about "the kingdom of heaven," while John's Gospel prefers "eternal life." Two of the apostle Paul's letters, 2 Corinthians and Galatians, refer to a "new creation." The letters to the Ephesians and to the Colossians refer to God's work in Christ to "gather up all things in him" and to "reconcile to himself all things." The book of Revelation refers to "a new heaven and a new earth." Each of these phrases emphasizes something a bit different, and the sheer variety should make us somewhat cautious about speaking too definitively about the mechanics of God's future activity. But in their own ways, all of these phrases point to God's work of healing what has gone wrong in creation and drawing us ever deeper into the love of God. And it is clear that we live in between two decisive moments in the history of God's saving work. We live two millennia after the life, death, and resurrection of Jesus Christ, and yet we still await and pray for the coming of God's kingdom in all its fullness.

The second thing to notice is the astonishing variety of ways in which the Christian tradition has tried to make sense of what Scripture says about the kingdom of God and its related concepts.

Some people have insisted that God's kingdom is a future reality, while others have emphasized its present dimensions. Some have stressed God's activity in bringing the kingdom, while others have focused on the calling of human beings to live in ways that help usher it in. Many see the kingdom of God as primarily an individual and spiritual reality, while others insist that it is a social reality. (Howard A. Snyder offers an extensive treatment of the various approaches to the kingdom of God in his book *Models of the Kingdom.*) In emphasizing certain aspects of God's kingdom, advocates of these views are drawing upon different passages of Scripture. For example, consider two passages from the Gospels that reflect Jesus' teaching about the kingdom of God. The first is Luke 17:20-21: "Once Jesus was asked by the Pharisees when the kingdom of God was coming, and he answered, 'The kingdom of God is not coming with things that can be observed; nor will they say, "Look, here it is!" or "There it is!" For, in fact, the kingdom of God is among you.'" Jesus seems to indicate here that in some sense the kingdom is a present reality. (The New Revised Standard Version of the Bible notes an important alternate translation: "the kingdom of God is among you" could also be rendered "the kingdom of God is within you." While that is a very important difference with regard to the question of whether the kingdom is primarily a personal or a social reality, for our purposes it's worth recognizing that both options present the kingdom as a present reality rather than a future reality.) Yet in Mark 10:23, we read: "Jesus looked around and said to his disciples, 'How hard it will be for those who have wealth to enter the kingdom of God!'" And, of course, in the Lord's Prayer we pray for God's kingdom to come (whether we follow Matthew's version or Luke's version). So there is also an expectation for the full completion of the kingdom of God in the future.

Wherever you place the emphasis, there is general agreement

on this: the kingdom of God in its completeness is not yet here, but we can participate in it in some sense now. You can turn to other passages from the Gospels to see both of these ideas reflected at the same time. In Luke 18:17, for example, Jesus says: "Truly I tell you, whoever does not receive the kingdom of God as a little child will never enter it." In that statement, Jesus seems to suggest that the kingdom is both something to be received in the present and to be entered into in the future. Or look at Mark 4, where Jesus uses a number of farming parables to teach about the kingdom of God. Each of these parables implies that the kingdom of God is something that grows and develops; it is present as a seed and as a growing plant before it is finally complete. With all of this in mind, I believe that you can say with confidence that the kingdom of God is indeed related to — but certainly not completed by — your life and your work in the present world.

Still, you might want to ask: How much continuity is there between what I do now and God's complete and final kingdom? Can all of the sorts of work involved in the preceding examples of missional calling have eternal and lasting significance? I think you could make two mistakes here. One mistake would be to suppose that it is *solely through your efforts* that the kingdom of God is gradually brought to completion. You should always keep in mind that God is the one who brings the kingdom, and your participation in that work is a gift of grace. Sometimes you might not fully comprehend the way in which your work is used by God in contributing to the kingdom. Consider one of those farming parables told by Jesus, in Mark 4:26-29: "The kingdom of God is as if someone would scatter seed on the ground, and would sleep and rise night and day, and the seed would sprout and grow, he does not know how. The earth produces of itself, first the stalk, then the head, then the full grain in the head. But when the grain is ripe, at once he goes in with his sickle, because the harvest has come." The role of the farmer is limited but crucial. And while he does not know precisely how the grain grows, the parable's implication is that the mysterious work of God brings the farmer's efforts to fruition.

The other mistake you could make presses in the other direction. You might suppose that evangelism is really the only work you can do that contributes to the kingdom of God. In this way of thinking, acts of service that improve life for people are good and useful but ultimately of only temporary significance. But I would suggest instead that Jesus' own pattern of ministry and teaching doesn't allow for such a chasm between the conditions of this life and the kingdom of God. At the beginning of Mark's Gospel, Jesus begins proclaiming the good news in Galilee that "the kingdom of God has come near" (1:14). As Jesus preaches this message, he also heals a number of people who are sick and casts out demons throughout the first chapters of Mark. There is a consistency between his words and his actions in these chapters, indicating that the restoration of wholeness in this life is very much related to the kingdom that he is proclaiming. This even comes through in his teaching ministry. Consider the parable of the Good Samaritan in Luke 10:25-37. Jesus tells this parable in response to a lawyer who is questioning Jesus about what he must do to inherit eternal life. The lawyer has rightly discerned that part of what is needed is to love his neighbor as himself, and — legal minds being what they are — he wants a clear and precise stipulation of just who his neighbor is. Jesus responds by telling the story of a man who takes care of someone who has been badly beaten, restoring him back to health. The implication is that a concrete act of caring for the needs of another does indeed have eternal significance.

How should you think about the relationship between such actions of service and the kingdom of God? I think the best way to conceive such acts is as a foretaste or a glimpse of the kingdom of God right in the midst of our present world. Just as Jesus' works of healing and casting out demons coincided with his teaching about the kingdom, so also your efforts to make life more whole for others in this life give you a tangible anticipation of life in the new creation. So Mother Teresa caring for people in poverty or a research scientist working to find a cure for cancer each contributes to God's kingdom in one particular sense. Presumably there will not be poverty or cancer in heaven, and the reason will not be because of the work of Mother Teresa or the research scientist — it will be entirely due to God's restoring work. But the tangible love expressed in these acts of service provides a foretaste of the ultimate victory of God's kingdom. In the same way, Jesus' healing miracles did not eliminate disease from history, but they did provide a visible sign of life in the kingdom of God. This is precisely the sense in which your missional calling is connected to God's reconciling work, even if it involves something other than evangelism.

Therefore you can be confident that God will use your efforts in this life in whatever manner God chooses. Like the farmer in the parable, you don't really know in advance how God will do that or what the result will be. But our exploration should be enough to make it clear that it is appropriate to speak of missional calling as oriented toward God's kingdom. In light of this, it is worth remembering two final things. First, not all missional callings involve the sort of service that has been considered in this section. All have a responsibility to love our neighbors in tangible ways, but for some missional calling will indeed involve evangelism, or prayer, or teaching the Christian tradition. Second, no matter what your missional calling, all believers are also called to explicit Christian proclamation and worship at appropriate times. (I will explore this in the discussion of general calling in Chapter Three.) Just because you have identified a particular missional

16

calling does not mean that you should neglect other dimensions of the Christian life. The kingdom that Jesus proclaimed was both a physical and spiritual reality, and he embodied it by both words and actions. His disciples are called to nothing less.

Missional Calling and the Bible

Let's ask one final question at the conclusion of this chapter. Is the notion of missional calling biblical? That is, has what has been said about this idea so far been shaped by experience alone, or is there something in the witness of Scripture that would lead Christians to embrace this idea? The first thing to acknowledge is that there are, quite simply, more examples of direct calling and general calling in Scripture than there are of missional calling. You will see plenty of examples of such passages in the next two chapters. Still, it would be a mistake to conclude that the idea of missional calling has no basis in the Bible. In fact, I would suggest that the best way to think of this relationship is that missional calling is a theological concept that helps us to make sense of a great deal of Scripture's witness.

In this light, it is somewhat similar to the way in which the doctrine of the Trinity relates to the Bible. We can certainly recognize the seeds of that doctrine in Scripture, such as the naming together of the Father, the Son, and the Holy Spirit in Matthew 28:19. But it would be too much to say that the full-blooded doctrine of the Trinity (as expressed in the Nicene Creed, for example) is explicitly outlined in the biblical texts. It took the church some three and a half centuries of prayerful reflection and debate on those texts to develop that doctrine. Along the way, there were plenty of ideas about God that were proposed by people reading the very same Bible that were ultimately found to be problematic. And the process of rejecting these ideas helped the Christian church to refine its doctrine of the Trinity further. In doing so, a body of teaching about God emerged that helped to make sense of the way Scripture talked about God's nature and activity. Alister E. McGrath, in his book *Theology: The Basics*, describes this development as follows:

> The best way of understanding the basis of this seemingly baffling doctrine is to consider it as being the inevitable and legitimate way of thinking about God which emerges from a sustained engagement with the biblical witness to the words and works of God. The doctrine of the Trinity can be regarded as the outcome of a process of sustained and critical reflection on the pattern of divine activity revealed in Scripture, and continued in Christian experience. This is not to say that Scripture contains or sets out an explicit doctrine of the Trinity; rather, Scripture bears witness to a God who demands to be understood in a Trinitarian manner. (p. 117)

So here is a case where a key idea in the Christian faith is not described in detail in the Bible, but it makes many key pieces of Scripture fit together in a way that no alternatives can.

While the doctrine of the Trinity is a central teaching of the classical Christian faith, the concept of missional calling certainly does not rise to that status. Still, the relationship between the idea and the witness of Scripture in both cases is similar. I am proposing that the category of missional calling can help people come to terms with the Bible's vision of how God has created us, in light of Christian experience. In particular, I want to suggest that this idea fits together three main elements: 1) biblical texts on spiritual gifts, 2) biblical reflection on God's intimate knowledge of us as God's creatures, and 3) Scripture's implication of freedom when there is no direct calling. The description of missional call-ing in this chapter aligns with these biblical themes in a way that rings true to experience.

First, consider the theme of spiritual gifts. Any discussion of spiritual gifts rightly focuses on the New Testament letters at-tributed to the apostle Paul. Three passages from these letters are worthy of particular attention in this regard: Romans 12:3-8, 1 Corinthians 12:1-31, and Ephesians 4:4-16. All of these passages suggest that God has gifted us in distinct ways. Each gift is to be used in its own way in God's service, and each has a unique and important contribution to make. It is worth noting that all three of these texts use the image of "the body of Christ" to talk about the community of faith. The different parts of the body represent different gifts that are used as we work together toward Christ's purposes. For example, we might look at Romans 12:4-8:

> For as in one body we have many members, and not all the members have the same function, so we, who are many, are one body in Christ, and individually we are members one of another. We have gifts that differ according to the grace given to us: prophecy, in proportion to faith; ministry, in ministering; the teacher, in teaching; the exhorter, in ex-hortation; the giver, in generosity; the leader, in diligence; the compassionate, in cheerfulness.

One thing that is especially striking in these passages is that the specific list of gifts is different in each case. There is some overlap, to be sure, but none of the lists are identical. The point of these texts, then, does not seem to be that Christians need to agree upon a finite and official set of spiritual gifts that are recognized in the church. Rather, the emphasis is on looking to the specific way that the Holy Spirit has gifted each person to find his or her unique contribution — and to appreciate the unique contributions of everyone. That is precisely what missional calling is about.

A second biblical theme that aligns with the idea of missional calling is God's intimate knowledge of God's creatures. The idea that work should align with the unique way in which God has created each person is embraced in both the Old Testament and the New Testament. One of the best-known texts in the Bible, for example, is Psalm 139. Consider the connection between God's creative activity and the life of the Psalmist in verses 13-16:

> For it was you who formed my inward parts;
>   you knit me together in my mother's womb.
> I praise you, for I am fearfully and wonderfully made.
>   Wonderful are your works; that I know very well.
>   My frame was not hidden from you,
> when I was being made in secret,
>   intricately woven in the depths of the earth.
> Your eyes beheld my unformed substance.
> In your book were written
>   all the days that were formed for me,
>   when none of them as yet existed.

The notion that God created the Psalmist — and by implication, you — with such intricate detail and knowledge is reason for celebration and praise. And God has given you the gift of time, has formed your days, so that you can give expression to the uniqueness of God's handiwork in your contributions to God's purposes. In the New Testament, turn to Ephesians 2:10: "For we are what he has made us, created in Christ Jesus for good works, which God prepared beforehand to be our way of life." While this text appears to refer collectively to all of God's people, the passage on spiritual gifts in Ephesians 4 (from the very same letter) is a reminder that this work takes shape differently according to each person's gifts. The connection of God's deep knowledge of you and the distinctive shape of your life's contribution is made clearly when you think in terms of missional calling.

Sometimes passages like Psalm 139 and Ephesians 2:10 lead people to assume that God has planned out every detail of their lives. That is, for every decision or possibility that confronts you, God has one "right" possibility that represents God's will. This leaves every other possibility as a wrong choice, one that takes you outside of God's will and displeases God. Even though such a view is quite common, I would suggest that both Scripture and experience present a very different picture. While it is certainly true that there are times when God wants something specific from you — this is what the next chapter of this book is about — there are also times when God gives you tremendous freedom. I have spoken with many people in the midst of making some major decision: Should I major in biology or art? Should I marry this person or not? Should I transfer to another university or stay here? Many times, even after seeking a clear answer from God through prayer, reading the Bible, conversations, and plenty of anxiety, no clear answer comes. Or, to put it more precisely, the answer seems to be: *You can be within God's will or outside God's will by taking either path, depending on how faithfully you live as you go down that path.* Sometimes there is no direct calling, even when you would like one. And in those cases, what matters most is how you live for and serve God in the context of whatever choice you have made. Jerry Sittser nicely demonstrates the problems with the "conventional approach" to God's will and offers a lucid account of our freedom in *The Will of God as a Way of Life*. In his words, you have "astonishing freedom" to live out God's will in whatever circumstances you find yourself (pp. 22-40).

Many passages of Scripture affirm this very kind of freedom.

Indeed, this is the third biblical theme that fits together in the idea of missional calling. Consider how James 4:13-16 talks about God's will: "Come now, you who say, 'Today or tomorrow we will go to such and such a town and spend a year there, doing business and making money.' Yet you do not even know what tomorrow will bring. What is your life? For you are a mist that appears for a little while and then vanishes. Instead you ought to say, 'If the Lord wishes, we will live and do this or that.'" Now, on the one hand, it is clear that the main point of the passage is that your plans don't decisively determine the future. But the striking thing is that the text still encourages you to make plans and make choices even as you lack control over the future. Too often, you may be afraid to take a single step until you hear a decisive direct calling from God. Yet this passage suggests just the opposite: You should move forward in humility, making the best choices and plans that you can. As you step ahead in this freedom, you still have the responsibility to live faithfully according to God's calling. Colossians 3:17 offers this kind of focus on the *how* rather than on the *what*: "And whatever you do, in word or deed, do everything in the name of the Lord Jesus, giving thanks to God the Father through him."

The idea of missional calling, then, draws on these biblical themes to address a space that you may often find in your life. How do you serve God when you do not discern a specific task or choice that God wants you to make in this particular instance? You do so by living out your general calling (more on that in Chapter Three) and by living out your missional calling by any means you can find in your present circumstances. God has given you particular gifts to be used in their own way. And God has crafted you in intricate detail, enabling a distinct contribution that you can make to glorify your maker. So you can get to work, by God's grace and in the power of the Holy Spirit, to make that unique contribution. Wherever you are and whatever limitations you might face in the present, there is a way that you can play your part in providing a glimpse of God's kingdom. As you do so, joyfully and with the grain of your being, you are living out your missional calling.

DISCUSSION QUESTIONS

1. Think about how you've understood the phrase "finding your vocation" in the past. How does the idea of missional calling compare to that?

2. Do you currently feel a sense of mission or purpose that gives shape to your life? If so, how would you describe that mission?

3. Have you often thought that God has only one right answer to every decision you might make — about where to go to school, what career path to take, whom to marry? If so, where do you suppose this idea came from?

4. How do you respond to the idea that we have freedom to choose among multiple paths in those times when we do not sense a direct calling from God?

5. What are some ways in which your life right now provides a glimpse of God's kingdom?

2

Is That You, Lord?
The Concept of Direct Calling

Late at night, as he was drifting off to sleep, young Samuel heard the voice of God (see 1 Samuel 3). To all appearances, this is not something that he or anyone else might have expected. For one thing, Samuel lived at a time in Israel's history when it was not very common to hear directly from God. "The word of the Lord was rare in those days," we are told in 1 Samuel 3:1; "visions were not widespread." For another thing, as a boy serving the priest Eli at Israel's holy site of Shiloh, Samuel was not the first person we would expect to hear directly from the Lord. If God were to speak to anyone in those days, we might suppose that the priest would be the one to hear it. We might note that Eli did hear a prophetic word from the Lord, though indirectly, in 1 Samuel 2:27-36. In that case, a "man of God" came to Eli and delivered the (rather unpromising) message. But it was the boy Samuel, lying there in the temple of the Lord, whom God addressed by name.

When he heard his name called, apparently in an audible voice, he repeatedly mistook it for the voice of Eli. Three times he ran into the priest's room to see what Eli wanted. Finally recognizing what was happening, Eli sent Samuel back into the temple with instructions: "Go, lie down; and if he calls you, you shall say, 'Speak, Lord, for your servant is listening.'" When Samuel did just that, God responded with a blistering prophetic message against Eli's family. As we might imagine, Samuel was quite frightened by what he heard and did not want to reveal the message to Eli. But after some prompting from the old priest himself, Samuel told Eli everything. From that time on, the Lord would continue to speak to Samuel — and to all Israel through him.

Many of you, probably most of you, will never hear an audible voice from God in the way that Samuel did. And you should always be careful about how you take narrative material in the Bible like 1 Samuel and apply it to your own life. Still, there are two things about this narrative that are especially striking and, I would suggest, quite relevant to your own understanding of calling. First, though God called Samuel's name directly, Samuel needed help to understand what was going on. He needed the help of community — in the form of the priest Eli — to perceive that it was God who was calling to him. Second, despite the many failures of Eli's family and the lack of spiritual sensitivity among those surrounding Samuel, God did indeed get through to the boy. Eli himself was capable of mistaking Samuel's devout mother at prayer for someone who had had too much to drink (see 1 Sam. 1:9-16). Yet he was still able to play a crucial role in confirming that Samuel was indeed hearing from God.

The narrative of young Samuel in the temple is a very important one as you consider the second category of calling, *direct calling*. As I noted in the Introduction, instances of direct calling involve specific tasks that God directs individuals to do. While there was no explicit task that God asked of Samuel, one was certainly implicit — he was to give the prophetic message he had received to Eli. And the message itself was quite clear. Once Samuel had established, with Eli's help, that God was speaking to him, there was little doubt about what God was communicating. The question was not *what* the calling was, but rather *whether* it was truly from God and *whether* Samuel would be obedient. This is a telltale mark of direct calling.

Features of Direct Calling

To develop an account of direct calling as it might occur in your own life, let's focus once again on five basic features. First, *a direct calling may not necessarily align with our gifts.* While we saw in Chapter One that missional calling usually does connect closely with how God has gifted us, that is not always the case in instances of direct calling. Many of the call stories in the Bible reflect this reality very clearly. Perhaps the most famous example is the one that we explored in the Introduction: the calling of Moses in Exodus 3-4. Speaking out of a burning bush, the Lord tells Moses of the plan to rescue the people of Israel from oppression in Egypt: "I will send you to Pharaoh to bring my people, the Israelites, out of Egypt" (Exod. 3:10). Clearly unsettled by what he hears, Moses tries to convey to God that he is completely unfit for this task. "O my Lord, I have never been eloquent, neither in the past nor even now that you have spoken to your servant; but I am slow of speech and slow of tongue" (Exod. 4:10). The response Moses receives from the Lord is interesting in two respects. First, God does not challenge Moses' assertion that he is ill prepared for the task. Second, despite this, God does not withdraw the calling. On the contrary, by claiming to be the one who gives speech to human beings in the first place, the Lord insists that Moses will be empowered to fulfill the calling he has been given(Exod. 4:11-17).

This story is just one example of a common biblical theme: when there is a task to be done, God calls whomever God chooses. God is not limited by your particular sets of gifts and abilities. As in the case of Moses, God is free to use someone who feels — and who may in fact be — quite unprepared for a specific task. Again, you should remember that your gifts are central to understanding the long-term, sustained pattern of contribution to God's kingdom that I have been identifying as missional calling. But the point here is that God remains free to direct you to tasks that do not align with your missional calling. The seminary professor who spends her career cultivating theological precision among knowledgeable Christians may feel led to do something quite different — say, to share the gospel with the passenger next to her on an airplane. Though she feels intimidated by this idea and does not find that it comes naturally to her, she is faithful and trusts God to work through her. This kind of situation is a good example of a direct calling. Though missional calling and direct calling are two very different kinds of vocation, they both depend on the same theological conviction. Your ability to respond faithfully to God's calling comes from God, whether by means of the particular and sustained gifts God has given you or by God's enabling you to fulfill a task that may not be a natural fit for your gifts. "Who gives speech to mortals?" the Lord asks Moses. "Is it not I, the Lord? Now go, and I will be with your mouth and teach you what you are to speak" (Exod. 4:11-12). Read Jeremiah 1:4-10 for another powerful example of such an exchange when Jeremiah receives his call to be a prophet.

A second characteristic of a direct calling is that it *may not necessarily align with your passions or give you joy.* This is another area of considerable difference between missional calling and direct calling. As noted in Chapter One, missional calling tends to go with the grain of the passions that God has given you. But you must recognize that God is free to ask things of you that, quite frankly, you may not want to do. It is one thing to say that God created you in such a way that you can and should find joy in

27

your long-term missional calling. It would be quite another thing to suggest that God only calls you to tasks that you love — in fact, such a suggestion runs counter to the ways in which Scripture tends to depict calling. Jonah's direct calling to go to Nineveh unnerved him so much that he immediately got on a ship so that he could "flee to Tarshish from the presence of the Lord" (Jon. 1:3). Though Jonah ran from the calling that the Lord had placed upon his life, God did not withdraw that calling simply because Jonah didn't want to do it.

The New Testament makes it clear that there is considerable cost in following Jesus. While the path of discipleship is life-giving and fulfilling in the deepest sense, his followers are given no promise that life will always be easy or free of pain. On the contrary, those who wish to be Jesus' disciples are called to "deny themselves and take up their cross and follow me" (Mark 8:34). This often involves specific cases of direct calling that do not at all reflect what his disciples want. In Mark 10, Jesus directs a wealthy man to sell his possessions, give the money to the poor, and then to follow Jesus. "When he heard this, he was shocked and went away grieving, for he had many possessions" (v. 22). As difficult as it may be, though, obedience in instances of direct calling is simply part of walking the way of the cross as a disciple of Jesus. And Jesus makes it clear that his followers will be empowered by the Holy Spirit to do what they have been called to do. When he tells the disciples that they will face persecution because of their obedience to him, for example, he offers these words of reassurance: "When they bring you to trial and hand you over, do not worry beforehand about what you are to say; but say whatever is given you at that time, for it is not you who speak, but the Holy Spirit" (Mark 13:11). Once again, you can be assured that God enables the fulfillment of direct calling.

Not only does a direct calling potentially involve doing something you dread, but you may also find that it takes you away temporarily from what you love to do. In his memoir of vocation *Now and Then,* Frederick Buechner notes that Gerard Manley Hopkins burned all of the poems he had previously written when he entered the Jesuit novitiate. Hopkins did so because he feared they would interfere with the specific vocation that God had placed upon his life. Buechner's point does not seem to be that the permanent destruction of the work of such a talent was necessarily a good idea. (In fact, by way of contrast, Buechner notes that he set aside his own unfinished novel "not so much as scorched" [p. 11] when he entered seminary in the 1950s). Rather, the point seems to be that Hopkins recognized that even good and joyful work needed to be put aside for a time in order to respond to a direct calling. While Hopkins — and Buechner, for that matter — ultimately returned to writing, the story can be a reminder that you do not have an irrevocable right to do whatever makes you happy. Work that gives you joy is a gift from God, and to find opportunities for such work is a good thing. But a direct calling may require that you set aside even such good work for a time. The concept of direct calling is a reminder that, while obedience and joy are not mutually exclusive, obedience to God must always take priority.

Third, in cases of direct calling *you will usually have little doubt about what is being asked of you, yet there is still a need for confirmation that the call is from God.* In the most famous call stories of the Bible — Abram, Moses, Isaiah, Jeremiah, Ezekiel, Levi, and Saul, among others — it is remarkable to see how clearly these people understood what God wanted of them. In each of those stories, God (Jesus in the latter two cases) initiated the call and made it very clear what was being asked. While many of us have not experienced a direct call to pick up and move to a new land, as Abram did, I suspect that most Christians have experienced times when they clearly sensed God leading them to do something specific. The actual means of calling can vary — it might come through a conversation with other people, through an internal sense of God's leading, or through a literal or figurative dream. However it comes, many Christians experience a sense that God is directing them to talk to a particular person, to cut something out of their life, to begin mentoring at a local youth center, or to any number of other possibilities. Such a calling may take you outside of your comfort zone, but in these instances there is generally a very strong awareness of what God is asking of you.

History and experience have shown, however, that not everyone who thinks he or she is hearing from God is in fact hearing from God. In some cases, the voices of a surrounding culture or of one's own desires might be mistaken for the voice of God. Self-deception is a genuine possibility. In other cases, psychological or emotional turmoil might render one's spiritual senses less than perfectly reliable. For these reasons, it is crucial for you to examine instances of direct calling with the help of the community of faith. "Beloved, do not believe every spirit," reads 1 John 4:1, "but test the spirits to see whether they are from God; for many false prophets have gone out into the world." The point is not to undermine the reality of direct calling from God, but rather to do what you can to confirm that you are not confused or deceived in such cases.

At this point, I would like to introduce a distinction in terminology that I will be using throughout the remainder of the book; namely, the distinction between *discernment* and *confirmation*. I am not suggesting that everyone uses these terms in the manner that I am using them. On the contrary, there is significant overlap and fluidity in the common uses of these terms. I do suggest, however, that there is a conceptual difference between what I am calling discernment and what I am calling confirmation, and terminological consistency will help to keep that difference clear. As I suggested in Chapter One, your missional calling is usually not immediately evident. In general, it takes considerable time, prayer, and communal engagement to determine what shape your sustained contribution to God's kingdom will take. I will use the term *discernment* to specify this often-messy process of discovering your missional calling. By contrast, as I have been arguing, cases of direct calling tend to be rather clear. You do not initiate such calls; rather, God does. But even a clear sense of direct calling should be treated with care, if you take the caution of 1 John seriously. In that light, I will use the term *confirmation* to refer to the work of examining a particular claim of God's leading to see whether it is from God. I will say more in what follows about both of these processes.

Fourth, *instances of direct calling vary significantly in duration and scope.* Some are very short-term and involve little immediate disruption of one's life. For example, you might see someone in a hospital lobby who looks very distraught. If you sense a clear and relentless prompting of the Holy Spirit to walk over and talk to that person, you could rightly think of that as a case of direct calling. While it's possible that such a conversation might result in a life-changing experience for both of you, it's reasonable for you, when you feel this prompting, to suppose that obedience in this case will not require turning your life upside down. This does not make obedience any less important, of course. But it does suggest that there are instances of God's particular calling that occur within the course of daily life and which are not completely uprooting.

Other cases of direct calling might be much more demanding. Let's suppose a successful middle school principal, for reasons unknown to her, begins to recognize God putting the people of Burundi on her heart. (While there are many elements in this example that reflect people I have known, this is an example that I have constructed.) She happens to read a profile of life in Burundi in a magazine. She has recurring dreams of sitting in an office looking out at children on a playground there. A guest speaker at her congregation tells of plans to build a school for children in that country. Not knowing what to make of all of this, she is startled when that same speaker calls her on the telephone later that week. The pastor gave the speaker her name, and they begin a conversation that ultimately leads to her being offered the job as principal of the new school in Burundi. Rather surprisingly to her, she begins to sense very strongly that God is leading her to accept the position. Thus, she begins a process of confirmation with her family and with members of her congregation. If through this process they determine together that God is indeed leading her to go, the move will result in a very different life for her. At this stage, she does not know how long she would be there, but there is a good chance that it might be for the rest of her working life. In cases such as this, obedience to direct calling requires a great deal more sacrifice and change than in the case of the hospital lobby. Yet in both cases, the appropriate way forward is obedience.

Fifth, *some people may have many experiences of direct calling in their lives, while others may have none at all.* The overriding theme in these reflections on direct calling is God's freedom. God is free to call whomever God wishes, when God will, and in the manner that God chooses. While this is true of missional calling as well, I suggested in Chapter One that people generally only have one missional calling that is sustained in different ways throughout their lives. Direct calling, on the other hand, is much more variable. It may or may not occur in your life. It may occur numerous times. It is certainly possible that multiple direct callings overlap in one person's life. To take the last two examples, there is no reason to suppose that the middle school principal called to Burundi might not also sense the kind of direct calling I described in the hospital lobby example. You simply do not know in advance how God may choose to speak into your life, but your attitude should be one of openness and readiness to respond.

Why is it that some people seem to experience a direct calling from God more than others do? I do not think we know, or even can know, the answer to this question. One might be tempted to suppose that it's because some people are more open to God's leading than others, that some have refined their spiritual senses more sharply. However, I would hesitate to make this sort of an argument to explain the variance in direct calling. It is true that the more mature you become as disciples of Jesus Christ, the better you will be at hearing and recognizing God's voice. And I certainly believe that you should always be aiming to cultivate your attentiveness to God in the midst of your daily lives. But this ongoing work of developing your spiritual senses is more immediately related to missional calling and general calling (which we'll explore in Chapter Three) than to direct calling. Cultivating a close relationship with God enables you to recognize ways to live out your missional calling as well as your general calling in the changing circumstances of your lives. You should never allow yourself to become passive in your day-to-day faithfulness to God. But you must remember that direct calling is always a function of God's initiative, and Scripture suggests that God can reach you at any level of spiritual maturity. God is free to speak quietly out of the silence (see 1 Kings 19:11-13) or through a dramatic encounter with the risen Jesus (see Acts 9:1-9), but God's ability to get through to you is not dependent on your spiritual faculties.

The key point to remember here is that you do not need to go looking for a direct calling. You should indeed seek to discern your missional calling. And once you've identified that missional calling, you should always aim to find ways of living it out — along with your general calling — in the situations that you face. But a direct calling is something you need not worry about finding. If we take Scripture's witness seriously, then God will find you if there is a very particular place to go or task to be done. In my experience of working with university students, I have found that many of them experience considerable anxiety when they do not receive a clear word from God about where to go or what to do. In such times, it is helpful to remember that you can still live out your calling — both missional and general — by making wise choices about how to use your time, gifts, and energy. The absence of a clear direction from God is not license to do whatever you wish, of course. But there is significant freedom to make choices based on what God has given you in order to be faithful in whatever circumstances you might find yourself.

If you do sense a direct calling from God, remember that there is something that you usually need to seek: confirmation. And this is where the spiritual senses do play an important role in direct calling. When someone has a sense that God is leading him or her in a very specific direction, the ability to recognize that it is indeed the voice of God that one is sensing is absolutely crucial. This ability is not only important for the one perceiving the call, but also — perhaps especially — for others who are involved in confirming the call. Throughout your life, and particularly when you are new to the faith, it is essential to have mature voices around you who are experienced in the Christian life. Such people can help to affirm what you are sensing or, if necessary, to raise red flags about potential concerns. In short, those with well-developed spiritual senses can help you "test the spirits." We now turn to explore that process of confirmation.

The Confirmation Principle

As soon as you begin to consider the idea of confirming a claim to direct calling, an obvious question arises: How extensive does a confirmation process need to be? If I feel the prompting of the Holy Spirit to begin speaking to the person quietly crying next to me on the bus, is it really practical to call together a gathering of fellow Christians to be sure I'm really hearing from God? Even if I'm mistaking normal human compassion for the voice of God in that case (though the two are not necessarily at cross-purposes), there is little harm that could be expected to come from initiating a conversation. On the other hand, if a person believes she is sensing God's clear call to quit her job and being working on a graduate degree, the stakes are much higher. Doing so would mean giving up a regular income and benefits. It would leave significant unknowns regarding her future prospects for reentering the job market. And it is at least conceivable that she is mistaking a desire for change — heightened by frustration with aspects of her current job — for the call of God. In this case, the potential hazards are considerable. It would be very unwise to embark hastily on such a journey without prayerful, thoughtful counsel from others who are spiritually mature and who know her well.

These examples illustrate a basic guideline I would like to suggest regarding the extent of confirmation. You might call this the confirmation principle: *the greater the consequences of acting on a supposed direct calling, the more extensive the confirmation process should be.* If responding to a sense of direct calling would significantly disrupt lives, put tension on a relationship, or jeopardize what someone has spent years building, then it is absolutely essential to involve others in thorough and prayerful confirmation. Precisely because it is possible to be mistaken in such cases, you should do all you can to make sure that what you think is from

God truly is from God. This is not only because of the pain and frustration that missteps can cause for yourself and for loved ones, though that would certainly be reason enough. It is also because following a direct calling can divert you from good and fruitful work that aligns with your gifts and passions. As we've seen, this diversion is a price you must pay if the direct calling is truly from God. But if you find that you have traveled down a wrong path because you were not careful to confirm what you thought was a direct calling, the good work you might have otherwise done with respect to your missional calling is lost. You simply do not want to find yourself grieving because you mistook your own desire for the voice of God and did not take the time and effort to "test the spirits."

Upon reading this, you might wish to raise an objection: Does not the confirmation principle undermine your sense of total commitment to God? Doesn't it put you in a position to obey God when it's easy to do so but resist God's call when it's demanding? The answer is an unqualified no. For the confirmation principle does nothing to reduce the demands of a genuine calling from God. God may indeed call you to a difficult task that involves sacrifice. If that happens, you really do need to obey. The confirmation principle is fully compatible with a total commitment to obeying God — in fact, it assumes such a commitment. Precisely because a true disciple of Jesus Christ stands ready to follow wherever God leads, it is a significant occurrence when that disciple believes that God is leading somewhere specific. Charging forward without carefully considering whether a call is genuinely from God is a sign of spiritual immaturity rather than commitment. And the greater the potential fallout if one gets it wrong, the more careful that consideration needs to be.

What, then, should such a confirmation process involve? What should be considered when you begin to assess a claim to direct calling? While there is no precise road map for confirmation, I would like to suggest three basic considerations. We get a clue to the first when we keep reading the passage cited earlier from 1 John 4: "Beloved, do not believe every spirit, but test the spirits to see whether they are from God; for many false prophets have gone out into the world. By this you know the Spirit of God: every spirit that confesses that Jesus Christ has come in the flesh is from God, and every spirit that does not confess Jesus is not from God" (vv. 1-3). The text points to Jesus Christ as a centering criterion for assessing claims to God's direction. This suggests that *following a direct calling should always be consistent with what God has revealed in and through Jesus Christ*. If a person claims that God is calling him or her to a task that is at odds with the example or the teaching of Jesus, then it is appropriate to conclude that the claim is mistaken. This is not to suggest that there is complete agreement in the Christian community regarding God's nature and purposes as revealed in Jesus. The issues of interpreting and privileging certain passages of Scripture remain with us, and it is possible that they will come up in discussions of confirming a direct calling. Nonetheless, the very first question you should ask in such discussions is whether the direction of a claim to God's leading aligns with God's nature and action as revealed in Jesus.

A second consideration in a process of confirmation is *the collective sense of a community of mature Christians together with the one perceiving the direct calling*. Gathering trusted people together to pray, to listen, and to ask questions regarding a supposed direct calling is a wise and time-tested practice. Such gatherings can provide perspective that one person — even one who is mature in the faith — cannot gain on his or her own. Fellow believers can help you identify possible ulterior motives, for example, that you might not have seen on your own. Or they might recognize that a person senses God leading in this direction only in particularly suspect situations — say, in times of serious sleep deprivation or when taking a certain medication. (This would not completely eliminate the possibility that the call is authentic, of course, but such patterns should at least be part of the conversation of confirmation.) Such a gathering can take many forms. Keeping the confirmation principle in mind, you may wish to consult one or two other people or convene a much more extensive community depending on the scope of the direct calling. The Quaker tradition has a longstanding version known as a "clearness committee," in which a small group of people ask honest, open questions to help someone gain clarity on a major question or decision. Parker J. Palmer offers a wonderful (and humorous) example of the value of a clearness committee in *Let Your Life Speak* (pp. 44-46). Whatever form a consultation may take, the wisdom of the community is a valuable part of confirming a significant direct calling.

It is worth noting, of course, that communal reflection is not foolproof — communities have been wrong at times, just as individuals have been wrong. For this reason, you will want to include participants in the confirmation process who have significant experience in the faith. God can certainly speak through new believers as well as through longtime disciples, but there is considerable value in listening to those who are a few steps further down the road than you are. It is also a good idea to seek as much diversity as possible in gathering a community of confirmation. Try to hear from those who are old and those who are young, from those who are naturally adventurous and those who are naturally cautious, and from those who are in different places on the theological spectrum. If you can, talk with those who regularly sense God speaking in very specific ways into their lives and with those who are more skeptical about such instances. Including conversation partners who are broadly representative of the community of faith will give you access to a variety of perspectives on how

God speaks and help you to see what you might not have seen on your own. Even though a communal process of confirmation offers no guarantees, including the wisdom of others is vastly better than going it alone.

Third, it is important to keep in mind the practices that help you to mature in the faith and gradually learn to recognize God's voice. *Regular engagement in the spiritual disciplines of the Christian tradition continually tunes your spiritual senses so that you're better able to distinguish between authentic and false claims to direct calling.* While there is no definitive or exclusive list of such practices, they include such things as prayer, reading Scripture, fasting, worship, and receiving the sacraments. A very fine introduction to the spiritual disciplines in the Christian tradition is Richard J. Foster's *Celebration of Discipline: The Path to Spiritual Growth.* Being immersed in these disciplines is important for all Christians, and their value is especially evident when a claim to direct calling emerges. When they have committed themselves to growing in their ability to recognize God's voice, both the one sensing the calling and those helping to confirm that calling will be in a much better position to do so.

An example from the world of social media can illustrate this. Most of you have seen instances when a friend unintentionally leaves a computer signed in to his or her Facebook or Twitter account. If a roommate or a spouse finds such an irresistible situation, what follows is usually predictable: a humorous post made to look like it came from the account-holder. Thus friends and followers of this person might find on his or her newsfeed: "I have the cleanest, most considerate, and best-looking roommate in the world — how ever did I get so lucky?" It's usually not long before friends of the account-holder recognize what has happened. Comments will emerge under the post with a friendly "left your account logged in again, didn't you?" Why is it that we so quickly recognize that the post was made by an imposter? (And why is the roommate, who may well be clean, considerate, and good-looking, not offended that more people didn't believe the post was genuine?) The reason is simple. Over time, we come to learn a close friend's manner of speaking — both what he or she is likely to say and the way he or she is likely to say it. When it strikes us that a particular statement (or Facebook post) just does not sound like our friend, what we're really recognizing is a disconnect between the statement and years of experience in the presence of that friend. Something similar happens when you spend years opening yourself to God's presence by means of practicing the spiritual disciplines. You come to recognize that a particular claim to God's leading just doesn't sound like the voice of God. Such concerns are not based merely in feelings or in prefabricated ideas about how God is supposed to act. On the contrary, they are based in years of experience spent consistently opening yourself to God in searching the Scriptures, prayer, and worship.

In any discussion of the spiritual disciplines, remember that it is God who is the agent of transformation in your life. That is, God is the one who shapes your spiritual senses to be able to recognize the authentic guidance of God. It is often tempting to use the image of physical exercise to explain how the spiritual disciplines function. However, I think that this image is quite misleading in one important respect. When you engage in physical exercise, the exercise itself sets off the physical processes in your body that transform you. The spiritual disciplines, on the other hand, cultivate attentiveness to God and open space in your soul for God to work. But the disciplines themselves are not what change you. As Richard Foster writes, "The Disciplines allow us to place ourselves before God so that he can transform us. . . . By themselves the Spiritual Disciplines can do nothing; they can only get us to the place where something can be done" (*Celebration of Discipline*,

p. 7). For this reason, you may prefer other terms in referring to such practices — "means of grace," perhaps, or "devotional practices." Whichever term you use, the key is to remember that you can only create space for God to work. You cannot summon or direct God to transform you on your terms or your timeline. In that light, you should not expect the spiritual disciplines to be a magic formula to enable you unerringly to confirm or reject a supposed direct calling. They help greatly toward that end, but there is always a dimension of mystery when you are relating to the living God.

I wish to offer one final word of caution with regard to confirmation. It is wise not to announce broadly a sense of direct calling before engaging in a confirmation process, and this is especially true when it involves those who have a direct stake in the substance of that direct calling. Such mistakes are, unfortunately, all too common when people interact with Christian institutions. For example, an applicant to a competitive degree program at a seminary or university may write in the application essay, "I strongly believe that God has called me to be in this program." Or an applicant for an appealing job at a nonprofit organization may suggest in a cover letter that "I am convinced that God has opened this job specifically for me." It is conceivable, of course, that God has called these people to those places. But to say such things as part of the application process is rather presumptive theologically, not to mention that it places those addressed in a very awkward position. (This is especially true if similar statements are made by fifteen different people for the same opening!) If in fact God is calling someone in such a specific way — and I suspect that most job openings and graduate slots are *not* filled by direct calling from God — then surely the organization making the decision has an important role in the confirmation process. Rather than helping the process, claiming direct calling in the midst of the process can only complicate it. Here, again, you will recognize God's freedom and persistence in the area of direct calling. If God indeed calls you to a particular task or place, then you can be patient in seeking confirmation in appropriate ways. You do not need to jump ahead — God will make a way forward where God has truly called you to go.

Direct Calling and the Ordained Ministry

Having explored the difference between missional and direct calling in these last two chapters, it is worth asking where we might locate a call to pastoral ministry among these categories. We expect those seeking ordination to have appropriate gifts for ministry, which might lead us to think that a call to become a pastor is best considered a missional calling. (I fully recognize that pastors and those who are ordained are not identical categories. For various reasons — usually in extraordinary circumstances — pastors of local congregations in some traditions may not be ordained. And, there are many, like me, who are ordained but who do not serve full-time as pastors of a church. Generally speaking, though, ordination is the church's formal way of affirming a call to pastoral ministry.)

Furthermore, most people who enter the ordination process expect to serve in pastoral ministry for the long term. Despite these factors, it is best to think of a call to pastoral ministry as a special variety of direct calling. While every Christian is called to ministry — various kinds of service that align with his or her gifts — *pastoral* ministry is a very particular ministry within the church. It involves the responsibility to proclaim the Word of God, provide pastoral leadership to the community of faith, and administer the sacraments. It is not enough to think that you would enjoy serving as a pastor or that you could probably do a good job in that role. You should move forward in seeking ordination only if you have sensed the direct call of God to do so. Given the influence that a pastor holds in people's lives, and the considerable consequences of how that influence is used, this is not a step to be taken lightly.

It is important that a call to pastoral ministry is both perceived by the one being called and recognized by the community of faith. These are often described as *internal calls* and *external calls*. An internal call is your own perception that God is calling you to pastoral ministry. This can come in a variety of ways. For some, it may begin with a comment from another person that continually comes to mind. For others, it might be an experience of service that God uses to begin drawing you toward pastoral ministry. As with other forms of direct calling, it is usually quite clear to the person being called — whether she or he likes the idea of becoming a pastor or not. In fact, seminary students often tell me that they "ran from" their calling to pastoral ministry for years before finally accepting that God was not going to relent. However it occurs, the presence of an internal sense of calling to pastoral ministry is essential for you to move forward.

Just because you sense God directing you to pastoral ministry, however, does not necessarily mean that such a call is present. You must remember the importance of confirmation through an external call. And keeping in mind the confirmation principle, the remarkably high stakes of serving in pastoral ministry mean that a very deliberate and extensive process of confirmation is necessary. Your gifts and fitness for pastoral ministry *as well as* a collective sense of God's direct calling must be affirmed by the community of faith in which you are to serve. Ordination is the traditional mark of such an external call. While different church traditions have different paths and processes for ordination, there is widespread agreement that such steps are necessary to affirm the call that the person has perceived — for the good of the person and for the good of the church. A nice example of an external call in action is the case of Barnabas and Saul in Acts 13:2-3.

Does the presence of spiritual gifts that align with pastoral ministry constitute a direct call? The best way to answer this question is to say that gifts for pastoral ministry are necessary but not sufficient. That is, part of the church's process of confirming a call to pastoral ministry is ensuring that a candidate has the appropriate gifts to serve in that capacity. But the mere presence of such gifts is not the same thing as an internal call. You may use such gifts in any number of ways appropriate to his or her missional calling. Most of us have encountered people who are serving God very faithfully in business, for example, who have gifts that we would also hope to see in a pastor. But if such a person has never felt God's distinct call to pastoral ministry, then it is neither necessary nor advisable for that person to consider becoming a pastor. God can and will use those gifts faithfully in whatever setting the person is in.

Finally, it is worth recalling something that we examined in Chapter One: You can live out your missional calling in the midst of pastoral ministry. That is, a direct call to become a pastor does not mean that your missional calling somehow disappears. On the contrary, the particular emphases of a pastor's work will be shaped by the contours of his or her missional calling. Some pastors will have a particular heart for urban ministry, while others will find that God has prepared them for rural ministry. Some will be particularly passionate about reaching those who are initially hostile to Christianity, while others will excel at deepening and enriching the faith of longtime Christians. Some will be consistently used by God to speak directly and prophetically against sin and injustice, while others will be particularly adept at extending

God's mercy and grace to those trapped in shame. Of course, at times, every pastor needs to work in ways that may not easily square with his or her missional calling. Pastoral discernment involves recognizing what is needed in a given situation, whether that comes easily to the pastor or not. But you need not set aside or ignore a missional calling when you receive a direct calling to pastoral ministry. And as anyone who knows a "retired" pastor can attest, his or her missional calling is continually expressed even after a pastor's formal career comes to an end.

Obedience, Freedom, and Peace

We have seen throughout this chapter that direct calling can take a variety of forms — long-term or short-term, desirable or undesirable, well-suited to your gifts or not. God may speak in a gentle whisper or through a howling wind. But if God calls directly, God gets through. And once you perceive and confirm a direct calling, the only right way forward is obedience. There is actually tremendous freedom in this realization. For those who receive a particular charge from God — demanding though it may be — there is no need to wonder about what to do next. When there is a collective peace among those involved in confirmation that a call is genuine, the path ahead is clear. In fact, one danger is that you might fear what God is directing you to do and thus extend the confirmation process as long as possible in order to avoid doing it. Such a delay tactic is as problematic in its own way as is charging ahead without confirmation. Involving trusted others in testing the spirits is necessary, but the time comes to act on what you have received from God. When that point is reached, faithfulness is shown through obedience.

There is another reason why there is freedom in understanding the category of direct calling. If you *don't* have a direct calling, then you do not need to be anxious about how to serve God. If you do not sense God leading you somewhere specific, if you do not see any writing in the sky — then many possible avenues of service are open to you. You can be faithful to God in ways that are appropriate to your missional calling. This involves making choices and, sometimes, setting off into the unknown. There are, without a doubt, better and worse choices, and you should seek wisdom in every step you take. But each moment of each day offers an opportunity to live out your calling. This is true of the missional calling, oriented as it is to your unique personality and abilities, and it is also true of the general calling that God gives to all of us collectively. In that light, Chapter Three takes up the category of general calling.

DISCUSSION QUESTIONS

1. Have you ever experienced an instance of direct calling in your life? What was that like?

2. Have you ever been frustrated from seeking a direct calling from God but not sensing one? Has reading this chapter helped to reduce that frustration?

3. What can go wrong if someone *believes* he or she is hearing a direct calling from God but actually is not? Have you ever seen or experienced a situation like that?

4. Who are some of the people you would invite to participate in a process of confirmation with you? Why would you choose them?

3

How Shall I Now Live?
The Concept of General Calling

As a faculty member at a Christian university, I find that student behavior often falls into one of two patterns. The first pattern involves the student who has difficulty selecting a major or deciding on a career path. He may begin as a first-year student with the intention to major in biology and follow the pre-med track. But after a brutal encounter with general biology or organic chemistry, he may wonder if God is calling him to major in business. After taking a business class or two, he decides that it is not the right path for him. He considers majoring in theology, as one of his professors had encouraged him in that direction. But he wonders if he should major in theology when he doesn't see himself working in a church-related career. He loved his introductory course in sociology, but his parents are unsure what sort of career he will be able to find if he goes that route. On and on it goes. As the time approaches when a decision needs to be made, the student becomes paralyzed with confusion and fear. In the meantime, he lets some of his assignments slip, doesn't get much sleep, and becomes rather short-tempered with his roommate. Deeply concerned about the choices to be made for the future, he finds himself miserable in the present.

The second pattern is typical of a student who is a planner. She enters college with a plan, say, to major in biochemistry. She wants to build a résumé so that she can apply to graduate school. Deeply motivated, she hopes to become a researcher and devote her career to cancer research. So she meets with her advisor in the first term to diagram out all four years of courses that she will take. She makes a calendar of assignments and labs for each term, including a schedule of what she will need to accomplish each day. As the work piles on, the stress level goes up. Between her volunteer work at a lab, her own classes, and her part-time job, she feels pulled in every direction. Knowing exactly what she needs to get done in a day, distractions become more and more frustrating. Her roommate's boyfriend is always in her apartment. Her friends from high school keep asking her to spend time with them. Her sister seems to have an emotional crisis every night that requires a Skype intervention. She knows exactly where she wants her life to go, but the distractions of the present keep her from getting there. She is riddled with frustration. Like the first student, she is miserable in the present because her mind is set on the future.

What is common to both of these patterns is a neglect of God's calling for life in the here and now. Ironically, by striving to respond to God's calling for the future, these students tend to miss the very real opportunities to serve God in the present. Or, if they reluctantly meet those needs, they feel distracted from the real work God is preparing them to do. In theological terms, we could say that people are forgetting the importance of their *general calling* when they fall into these traps. Again, general calling refers to those things to which God calls all people. General calling is not limited to certain times or places; it is what God wants of everyone all the time. It is lived out in the midst of the mundane details of every day. And when your eyes are focused only on the future, you can miss the enormous impact those details have on the shape of your life. In fact, Jerry Sittser suggests that attending to your general calling can actually help relieve the frustration you may feel in worrying about the big choices that lie ahead: "We simply need to do what we already know in the present. God has been clear where clarity is most needed. . . . Who we choose to become and how we choose to live every day creates a trajectory for everything else" (*The Will of God*, p. 25). Being faithful in the midst of the needs and demands of today prepares your way for a faithful tomorrow.

Features of General Calling

As you aim to understand God's desires for all people, you can begin by recognizing that *there are different ways to articulate general calling.* You can focus more broadly or more narrowly, depending on your purpose. For example, it is entirely appropriate to say that regular prayer is part of your general calling. You might also say, more broadly, that growing as a faithful disciple of Christ is your general calling. Regular prayer is one of the many things that help you grow as a faithful disciple of Christ, but it is certainly not the only thing. You would also want to include works of mercy, seeking justice, studying Scripture, participating in a community of worship, and other practices of spiritual formation. You would also want to find ways to live out your discipleship in various ways throughout your life — at work, with your friends, and with your family. Therefore, you may at times focus in on a particular aspect of general calling (like prayer), while at other times you may want to find ways of articulating in more general terms what God asks of all people.

When we speak more broadly, there will inevitably be some overlap. One person might state her general calling as a paraphrase of Jesus' words in Matthew 22:37-40: to love God with all we are and to love our neighbors as ourselves. Another person might favor the language of Matthew 6:33, suggesting that his general calling is to seek God's kingdom and righteousness before all else. We do not need to decide between these. We can recognize that much of what is involved in loving God and loving our neighbors is involved in seeking God's kingdom and righteousness, while letting the resonance of each passage do its work. Scripture speaks with a refreshing variety of tones and images; it does us little good to try to diminish this variety.

This leads naturally to a second feature of general calling. *You do not need to seek out or discern your general calling,* as Scripture offers a comprehensive and compelling vision of God's desires for all people. General calling has to do with the known rather than the unknown. If you pay attention to the ways Scripture witnesses to God's self-disclosure, you will find that God has been abundantly clear with regard to the kind of life God wants all of us to live. To take just one biblical example, Paul exhorts us to live joyfully, prayerfully, and thankfully in whatever circumstances we face, since that is God's will for us in Christ Jesus (1 Thess. 5:16-18). Or to take another example, Paul writes in Romans 12:18, "if it is possible, so far as it depends on you, live peaceably with all." Such statements of general calling can give you immediate guidance when you find yourself in the midst of, say, a frustrating conflict with a friend. Remembering these basic dimensions of the vocation of all Christians redirects your focus back to the patient, faithful work of daily discipleship.

Now you may begin to see more ways in which general calling is different from missional and direct calling. Generally speaking, you need to seek out your missional calling. For most people, that is a process that takes time, prayer, experience, and the help of a community of people. While Scripture provides essential guidance throughout this discernment process, you will not likely find a passage in the Bible that says: "Sarah Smith, your missional calling is to help increase literacy for high-risk elementary school children." (If you do, someone has taken too many liberties in translating from the Hebrew or Greek!) Yet there is abundant biblical material that reflects all Christians' general calling in very specific ways. Direct calling is more like general calling in the sense that you do not need to seek it out. But as we saw in Chapter Two, not everyone receives a direct calling. God is free to speak into people's lives when and how God sees fit, and you should not try to force God's hand. Vocational frustration often comes in those times when you have not yet fully discerned your missional calling and no direct calling is evident. In those times, your general calling is actually a great gift, as it provides guidance for how you are to live in the present. However clear or unclear you may be on what the future holds, you know what God wants of you right now.

A third aspect of general calling involves the role of other Christians. While your general calling is revealed through Scripture, *it must be taught and supported by the community of faith.* Too often, people forget the crucial place of the church in learning and understanding God's word. But on reflection, I suspect, you'll recognize that the community of faith has been essential to the reception of the Bible for just about all Christians. This happens formally, in sermons, lessons, and Bible studies. It also happens informally, in conversations with parents, friends, and pastors. Both the passages in Scripture that you are most familiar with and the ways you understand them have a lot to do with the spiritual company you keep. Many Christians know Proverbs 3:5-6 or John 3:16 by heart; I suspect relatively few know Zechariah 8:12 by heart. (Go ahead and look it up. It's worth reading!) If you think about why so many of us know certain passages so well, the mediating role of the church will become fairly clear. And this is not a bad thing. You cultivate your love for God's word as well as your understanding of it in relationship with other Christians. Of course, you can and should study the entire Bible, including the lesser-known passages. There are hidden riches throughout God's word. But it is important to do so in the context of a community that helps you to make sense of what you find.

While each of you comes to know your general calling through Scripture, there is still the question of doing it. Here again the company of other Christians is critically important in supporting you as you try to live out your general calling. It's not only that you learn Scripture in the context of community, but you also encourage and hold each other accountable to live out what it teaches. This reality was brought home to me very clearly during my first year of college. A group of men from my floor in the residence hall would meet each week to pray, read Scripture, and talk about our lives. We called the group "Spur," based on Hebrews 10:24: "And let us consider how we may spur one another on toward love and good deeds"(NIV). (The NRSV, which I usually quote, uses the word "provoke" rather than "spur." Thinking back on it, "Provoke" would not have been a promising name for a small group!) There were about eight regulars in the group, and a few others joined in from time to time as well. The structure was fairly informal, but the impact — for me at least — was monumental. We encouraged each other, held each other accountable, and prayed together. The importance of the group was not primarily in learning new things. While we did gather some new insights from each other, most of the things we talked about were things we already knew in one way or another. The real key was having a group of fellow Christians for mutual support as we tried to put those things into action in our lives. Though we never thought in these terms at the time, I now realize that the group was about living out our general calling.

I remember that first year in college as a wonderful time in my life. But there is no guarantee that doing God's will in the here and now will somehow make you immune from difficulties. In fact, you must keep in mind a fourth characteristic of general calling: *it carries no assurance that life will always run smoothly.* An inescapable tension runs through the Bible in this respect. On the one hand, you can recognize that the way of life to which God calls you is for your own good. Walking in that way of life cultivates peace, hope, and well-being so that you can flourish in whatever circumstances you might face. As the eighteenth-century evangelist John Wesley put it in his sermon "The Way to the Kingdom," "true religion, or a heart right toward God and man [sic], implies happiness as well as holiness. For it is not only righteousness, but also 'peace and joy in the Holy Ghost.'" At the same time, we live in a broken world that is marked by a great deal of evil, suffering, and misery. You should not expect that obedience to God will make you immune to these realities. "Peace and joy in the Holy Ghost" enable you to survive and even flourish in challenging circumstances, but you are given no easy escape from such circumstances.

The tension between well-being and adversity is perhaps best expressed in the books of the Bible collectively known as the Wisdom Literature. This material includes such books as Job, Proverbs, the Song of Solomon, and Ecclesiastes, as well as many of the Psalms. A careful reading of these texts reveals both sides of the coin. In some of these texts, you will find a clear affirmation that the most fulfilling and rewarding way to live is by doing God's will. For example, Psalm 1:6 tells us that "the Lord watches over the way of the righteous, but the way of the wicked will perish." The book of Proverbs is full of similar claims. In Proverbs 1:32-33, for instance, Wisdom calls out: "For waywardness kills the simple, and the complacency of fools destroys them; but those who listen to me will be secure and will live at ease, without dread of disaster." On the other hand, many other Wisdom texts suggest that life in a broken world complicates those types of statements. When the Lord spoke to Job out of the whirlwind, Job was not given an explanation for why his life had been torn apart even though he had been "blameless and upright" (Job 1–2, 38:1–40:2). In Ecclesiastes 7:15, the Teacher observes: "In my vain life I have seen everything; there are righteous people who perish in their righteousness, and there are wicked people who prolong their life in their evildoing." The Wisdom Literature as a whole thus speaks with a dynamic voice. (For a fine introduction to the Wisdom Literature in the Old Testament, see Roland E. Murphy, *The Tree of Life*.) Those who live out their general calling will yield fruit in their season (Psalm 1:3), but they have no guarantee of storm-free lives. Moreover, obedience should not be offered for the purpose of receiving temporal rewards, but rather as a faithful response to the love and grace of God.

Just as you are not guaranteed an easy road, you are also not promised that your general calling will always reflect a perfect fit with your gifts and passions. This leads to a fifth mark of general calling: *you should not neglect it because of a lack of giftedness or joy.* In this respect, general calling is like direct calling. All are called to a life of prayer, whether or not you discern that you have a particular gift for prayer. Each of us has a responsibility to bear good news to the world in both word and deed, whether or not you have the particular gift of evangelism. In the same way, you are not called to love God and your neighbor only if you feel like it. Rather, you are called to such love even when — perhaps especially when — it is difficult and painful. And it is clearly not always easy to love your neighbor. As Barbara Brown Taylor puts it in *An Altar in the World*, "I know that I have an easier time loving humankind than I do loving particular human beings. Particular human beings hug my bumper in rush-hour traffic and shoot birds at me when I tap my brakes. Particular human beings drop my carefully selected portabella mushrooms into the bottom of my grocery bag and toss cans of beans on top of them"(p. 27). Despite the challenges of fulfilling this general calling — be they minor annoyances or serious wrongs — the calling remains for everyone.

Why might your gifts and loves not always line up with your general calling? There are many times when they will. But you may also face many situations in which the movement of life around you does not fit neatly with the way of life God intends. In those times, your general calling might demand that you live in prophetic witness against the injustice or indifference around you. And to be completely honest, that can be incredibly difficult. It can be difficult because you may not want to go against the flow, and it can be difficult because you do not feel particularly equipped for the task. But regardless of how you feel, you can be confident that God enables you to do what God calls you to do in every situation. As we read in the benediction of Hebrews 13:20-21:

> Now may the God of peace, who brought back from the dead our Lord Jesus, the great shepherd of the sheep, by the blood of the eternal covenant, make you complete in everything good so that you may do his will, working among us that which is pleasing in his sight, through Jesus Christ, to whom be the glory forever and ever. Amen.

In that light, you are left with little excuse. Though you may not feel up to the task of living faithfully in an unfaithful world, the very power of God that raised Jesus from the dead is also at work in you. Empowered by God, you can indeed live in a way that is pleasing in God's sight.

There is another reason why your general calling might not align with what you love and what you do well. Not only does the surrounding culture often resist God's purposes, but so also does your own will. The reality is that general calling is as much about what God wants to do *in* you as what God wants to do *through* you. If your general calling always reflected what comes easily to you, transformation would never be necessary. But if you see in Jesus a life that reflects faithfulness and obedience, then you also can see that we all have a long way to go. And that will require change, which is not always easy. One of the places in Scripture where this idea is expressed most clearly is Philippians 2, where Jesus is lifted up as an example of self-sacrificial obedience (verses 1-11). The apostle Paul then gives the following exhortation: "Therefore, my beloved, just as you have always obeyed me, not only in my presence, but much more now in my absence, work out your own salvation with fear and trembling; for it is God who is at work in you, enabling you both to will and to work for his good pleasure." In those times when transformation brings fear and trembling, it makes all the difference to know that you do not work alone. God works in you so that you are able to be obedient. That work may not always be pleasant. Yet you can be confident that faithfulness to your general calling is directed toward God's "good pleasure."

Biblical Witness to General Calling

What portraits of general calling are found, then, in the Bible? To even begin to answer this very large question, we will need to narrow our focus. For the purposes of this discussion, let us concentrate on general calling as it pertains to those who are already committed to the Christian faith. I say this because a common use of the term "call" in Scripture has to do with the call to salvation.

You can see this especially in the New Testament letters — 1 Corinthians 1:9, 1 Corinthians 7:17-24, and 1 Peter 3:9 all use the term in this way. In some Protestant traditions, people tend to think first of the call to salvation when they hear the phrase general calling. In these traditions, general call — given to all people — is often differentiated from effectual call, which is given only to the elect. This is not how the term general calling is being used in the present discussion. To be sure, I would not want to draw too sharp a line between the call to salvation and the call to Christians to live a certain kind of life. In fact, Ephesians 4:1 blends these together nicely: "I therefore, the prisoner in the Lord, beg you to lead a life worthy of the calling to which you have been called." (Second Thessalonians 1:11 brings these dimensions of calling together in a similar way.) A complete vision of salvation will include living the kind of life reflected in your general calling. Still, given the focus of this book, let's explore those passages that are primarily addressed to those who have crossed the threshold of faith.

Another way in which we will limit our focus involves the texts that refer to the calling of the people of Israel. Because these texts refer to God's people collectively, you might be tempted to think of them in terms of general calling. However, given the discussion thus far, it is more accurate to think of Israel's particular vocation as an example of a collective direct calling. That calling had a critical and irreplaceable role in God's work of salvation, and we would not do justice to its particularity to think of it in terms of general calling. Paul's repeated references to Israel's calling in Romans 9-11 make this especially clear. In that light, our exploration of biblical texts on general calling will be directed elsewhere.

It should be clear by now that our analysis will need to do more than just examine biblical references to the term calling. As you have seen throughout this discussion, calling is a multivalent term. It is used in different ways in different contexts. On top of that, many of the most fruitful passages in terms of describing a general calling do not use the term at all. We will look for examples, then, of two sorts of biblical texts that articulate a general calling. First, let's examine some examples of texts that offer a *vision* of general calling. Such texts don't necessarily describe the specific practices or attitudes to which you are called. Rather, they describe a way of thinking about your general calling so that you might embody the appropriate response in whatever situation you face. Second, let's examine some examples of passages that specify the actual *content* of what you are to be or do, usually in the form of a list of exhortations.

One clear example of the first category is found in Matthew 22:34-40. The passage reads:

When the Pharisees heard that he had silenced the Sadducees, they gathered together, and one of them, a lawyer, asked him a question to test him. "Teacher, which commandment in the law is the greatest?" He said to him, "'You shall love the Lord your God with all your heart, and with all your soul, and with all your mind.' This is the greatest and first commandment. And a second is like it: 'You shall love your neighbor as yourself.' On these two commandments hang all the law and the prophets."

In alluding to the commands given in Deuteronomy 6:5 and Leviticus 19:18, Jesus does not go into detail about what love of God and neighbor entails in various situations. Rather, he provides a vision of general calling that can and should shape your approach to any circumstance. Of course, to learn what loving God and loving your neighbors actually means, you will need to go further. Naturally, you will look to other teachings of Jesus. You will reflect on other passages elsewhere in Scripture. You will look to the examples of others who reflect such love in their own lives. And unavoidably, you will need to be immersed over time in a community of faith where you engage in practices that deepen your capacity to love God and others in concrete ways. (Samuel Wells offers an extended development of this point in his book *Improvisation: The Drama of Christian Ethics.*) Yet as you walk that road, the two commands that Jesus recalls give a good orientation. If you aim to love God and love your neighbors in everything that you do, you are off to a good start.

A second biblical text that offers a vision of general calling is 2 Thessalonians 1:11-12: "To this end we always pray for you, asking that our God will make you worthy of his call and will fulfill by his power every good resolve and work of faith, so that the name of our Lord Jesus may be glorified in you, and you in him, according to the grace of our God and the Lord Jesus Christ." This is another passage that envisions the call to salvation to include a call to live a particular kind of life by God's grace. It is set in the context of a longer discourse about Christian hope, which offers comfort in the midst of suffering by reminding readers of the coming righteous judgment of God and the revelation of Jesus in his glory. In light of that future, Christians are called to live in such a way that they might be prepared to be in the presence of that glory (verses 5 and 10). Furthermore, the prayer of verses 11-12 provides a calling for the present; namely, that God might empower believers to reflect a measure of that glory now. "Every good resolve and work of faith" is done by God's power "so that the name of our Lord Jesus may be glorified in you." Here is a beautiful vision of general calling. Each day, by God's grace, you should aim to live in such a way that Jesus is glorified in you. As your life reflects his glory, it provides a glimpse of what will ultimately be revealed to all people at his coming.

Let us examine one more text in this first category. Romans

12:1-2 offers the following vision of general calling: "I appeal to you therefore, brothers and sisters, by the mercies of God, to present your bodies as a living sacrifice, holy and acceptable to God, which is your spiritual worship. Do not be conformed to this world, but be transformed by the renewing of your minds, so that you may discern what is the will of God — what is good and acceptable and perfect." Notice that Paul does not explain in these verses what God's will is. Rather, he describes how God's will might be known. God's will is known through a process of transformation. The process begins when you offer your whole self to God — it is striking that Paul refers to "bodies" rather than just hearts — as an act of worship. As you do so, you are changed in such a way that you no longer conform to the patterns of the world around you. The center of that transformation is the "renewal of our minds," which enables you to discern God's will in each and every situation. Thus Paul gives another portrait of general calling. You are to offer your entire self to God — not one hour on a Sunday, not 8:00 A.M. to 5:00 P.M. on weekdays, but your whole life. Doing so will bring forth a radical change in how your mind apprehends the world and God's purposes within it. Before you know what specific responses might be called for in various circumstances, you must make a prior commitment to give God everything. As you do, your mind is refreshed in such a way that "what is good and acceptable and perfect" will emerge clearly.

Later in that same chapter, Paul does go on to specify some of what will be discerned by a renewed mind. Verses 3-8 exhort readers to find their place within the body of Christ humbly and in accordance with their spiritual gifts. As we saw in Chapter One, this is a particularly important passage in relation to your missional calling. The extended reflections in Romans 12:9–15:13 then turn back to general calling. In fact, this section of the letter offers a nice initial example of the second category: those biblical texts that convey the actual content of general calling. For example, here are the marks that Paul outlines in 12:9-18:

> Let love be genuine; hate what is evil, hold fast to what is good; love one another with mutual affection; outdo one another in showing honor. Do not lag in zeal, be ardent in spirit, serve the Lord. Rejoice in hope, be patient in suffering, persevere in prayer. Contribute to the needs of the saints; extend hospitality to strangers. Bless those who persecute you; bless and do not curse them. Rejoice with those who rejoice, weep with those who weep. Live in harmony with one another; do not be haughty, but associate with the lowly; do not claim to be wiser than you are. Do not repay anyone evil for evil, but take thought for what is noble in the sight of all. If it is possible, so far as it depends on you, live peaceably with all.

A tall order, indeed! Yet you should recognize two things about this list of instructions. First, think of it as a gift that this text provides some real-life illustrations of what your general calling involves in the midst of your daily circumstances. Second, don't be surprised that this way of life appears to be at odds with life as you've known it. If indeed a renewal of the mind is necessary to recognize "what is good and acceptable and perfect," then you should not expect to find a description of business as usual. Your calling does not, as Paul says, shape you in the patterns of this world.

The church's life as an alternative community in the world is also at the heart of the letter of 1 Peter. While the instructions in Chapter 5 of 1 Peter are addressed primarily to leaders in the church, throughout Chapters 1-4 we find more lists of instructions for how all Christians might live faithfully in a world that doesn't always understand them. Let's consider 2:1-5, which offers another instance of the second category of general calling:

> Rid yourselves, therefore, of all malice, and all guile, insincerity, envy, and all slander. Like newborn infants, long for the pure, spiritual milk, so that by it you may grow into salvation — if indeed you have tasted that the Lord is good. Come to him, a living stone, though rejected by mortals yet chosen and precious in God's sight, and like living stones, let yourselves be built into a spiritual house, to be a holy priesthood, to offer spiritual sacrifices acceptable to God through Jesus Christ.

This short passage provides remarkable insight into what the life of faith involves. First, believers are called to take an active role in putting aside former ways of life — especially those that undermine community. The words are strong: "rid yourselves" of those habits that work against God's purposes of building a holy people. Second, your calling involves a commitment to continue to mature. As you are nourished in the faith, verse 2 suggests, you "grow into salvation." And clearly, this kind of growth does not occur in those who aim to be spiritual free agents. Rather, coming to Jesus means being made into a community. As we all grow closer to Jesus — who also did not conform to the ways of the world — we are "built into a spiritual house" together. In those times when you are tempted to think of general calling as a purely individual matter, it is wise to take another look at 1 Peter.

One final passage that describes the content of general calling is 1 Thessalonians 5:16-18. These verses together reflect one sentence in a longer list of exhortations from the apostle Paul (the longer list is found in 5:12-22). The sentence is brief but powerful: "Rejoice always, pray without ceasing, give thanks in all circumstances; for this is the will of God in Christ Jesus for you." Here we see the essence of general calling. Paul does not suggest that God's will is for you to find your way to new circumstances (though that may of course be necessary at times). Rather, Paul suggests that God's will for you is to live joyfully, prayerfully, and thankfully in whatever circumstances you might find yourself. This text serves as a reminder that your most important callings do not often make it onto the "to do" lists that adorn your workspace — though perhaps they should! Each day, God calls you to actions whose importance is more ultimate: rejoice, pray, and give thanks.

The passages we have explored in this section are just a start. They are nowhere close to a comprehensive list of biblical texts on general calling. They do give a good sense of both the broad vision and the specific content of the way of life that the Bible envisions for us. Still, it is a very helpful exercise to spend time immersed in Scripture, looking specifically for expressions of general calling. How does a given text articulate the way we are to live? Does it provide a vision of calling or does it give the actual content? Even more, you might try to identify those passages that you want to work on embodying in the present season of your life. Which ones do you want to keep fresh in your mind each morning, as a way of orienting your approach to the day? There is perhaps no better vocational practice than reflecting on Scripture with a particular eye to your general calling.

Indicators That General Calling Is Being Neglected

Even though you know your general calling, it is remarkable to consider how many things can distract you from doing it. Sometimes you may be conscious of a dimension of your general calling that you are neglecting — such as making consistent time for prayer, perhaps, or living peaceably with a roommate. But there are other times when you may not recognize, at least at a level that registers with you consciously, where you might be falling short. In that respect, it is helpful to be aware of some indicators that you might be neglecting your general calling. Just like the warning lights on the dashboard of a car that signal a need for immediate mechanical attention, these signs suggest that action should be taken in your life soon. Many people try to push it for "just a few more days" before going to the mechanic, and they often find that the long-term costs of waiting are significant. Hopefully, you will be more responsive to the indicators in your own life.

One key sign comes in the form of comments from other people. It is vitally important to pay attention when people say something about the way you are carrying yourself. This is especially true if you hear such statements from people you interact with daily or people who know you really well. These friends, family members, and coworkers are in a good position to recognize the sort of slow changes in attitude or disposition that can come from neglecting your general calling. I'm not referring only to comments specifically about your general calling. It's somewhat rare for people to use such direct terms, though it is wonderful to have accountability partners in your life who can challenge you in that way. More often, you will hear statements about the *consequences* of forgetting your general calling: "You seem edgy lately." "You don't seem to be yourself — is everything alright?" "I miss you — we haven't really talked in so long." While you might be tempted for any number of reasons to ignore such warning lights, it is very dangerous to do so. Particularly if a comment catches you by surprise, you are wise to stop and take stock of how faithfully your life is reflecting God's will in that particular season.

A second indicator emerges when you find yourself preoccupied with the future. As noted at the outset of this chapter, you can become so focused on where God might be leading you next that you forget to attend to where you are now. Looking forward is a natural human tendency. Children long for the days to move quickly as their birthday or Christmas approaches. Teenagers can't wait until they can drive. College students often feel that they'll be able to do a great deal for God just as soon as they graduate and get "out into the world." Adults look forward to their next promotion or to their next vacation. While this tendency is not entirely negative, you should be aware that it can turn your attention away from what is right in front of you. Your preoccupation with the future can also take the form of worry about what might happen down the road. The questions are usually unspoken, but they can haunt your conscious thoughts: What if I don't find a job? What if I don't meet someone? What will my life be about when my kids leave the nest? It's rarely helpful to try to eliminate such questions completely, and in some circumstances they can prompt you to take useful action in your life. But they become a warning sign when they get in the way of fulfilling your general calling in the present. When hopes and fears about the future begin to paralyze you, remembering God's will for today can bring tremendous freedom.

Sometimes it is not concern about the future that distracts you. Excessive worry about the wrong things in the present can also get in the way. A third symptom of neglecting general calling appears when your life is held captive by a busy schedule. There is an old saying that "misery loves company," and it seems to find expression in contemporary North American society as we share in the malaise of overly-scheduled lives. For some, talking and worrying about long to-do lists can get in the way of actually making progress on them. For others, there really are too many commitments to do them all well. The problem for general calling emerges when you find your life enveloped by endless urgent needs, leaving little or no room for those things that are truly important. Spouses may find that they are not making intentional regular time for each other, even though they both agree that their marriage is among their highest priorities in life. A parent considers her kids far more important than her job, and yet she notices that her responses to those kids typically include phrases like "maybe as soon as I get those reports done." A PTA president lists his faith as his highest value in life, but he consistently postpones intentional time with God until the rhythm of the school year slows down a bit. Most of us have had times in our lives when we can relate to this pattern. You can be sure that life is out of balance when the love of God and neighbor is edged out by the laundry and the DMV.

When you spot one of these warning lights, you might respond in any number of ways. Some are prone to defensiveness and denial, insisting that the problem rests entirely with factors beyond their control. They look to anything or anyone else to blame for their own lack of attentiveness. Others are inclined to respond immediately with guilt. They already feel bad enough about the symptom, whether it's a comment from a coworker, constant worry about the future, or a feeling of being swallowed up by the calendar. The realization that the root of the problem is your own neglect of general calling can add another layer of self-blame that effectively paralyzes you. And, just as with the indicator lights on the dashboard of the car, some will choose to ignore the signs and hope they go away on their own. Yet the point is not to assign blame, nor is it to eliminate the symptom without addressing the underlying issue. Rather, these signals can be taken as a kind of gift. They direct you back to your primary task as a disciple of Christ: to do the will of God *in the midst of all you face in the course of a day.* Instead of reading these as final judgments or failures, you can understand them as an invitation to a more balanced life. Thankfully, there are concrete steps that you can take to accept that invitation.

From Knowing to Doing:
General Calling as Daily Practice

It is one thing to be aware of your general calling; it is quite another to do it on a daily basis. When a warning light flashes in your life, there are ways to help remain mindful of God's will for you. One step you can take is to find ways to include reminders of general calling into the rhythms of each day. Some people are "sticky note" people. I am most certainly one of them. A very easy way for a mischievous colleague to throw my day off track would be to come into my office and remove the myriad sticky notes attached to my desk. While there may be a lack of organizational wisdom in opening myself to such a vulnerability, I know that I will pay attention to what's on my sticky note for the day. By including aspects of my general calling on my to-do list along with papers to grade and meetings to prepare, I will have consistent reminders of what is ultimately important. The reminder function of popular calendar software can be another helpful ally. Suppose a person is focusing on the portrait of general calling expressed in 1 Thessalonians 5:16-18, which we examined earlier. She might create a daily 10:00 A.M. reminder to appear on her computer screen to think of one reason to rejoice. A reminder for 1:00 P.M. might serve as a call to prayer. At 4:00 P.M., she'll see the reminder to give thanks to God for one specific blessing in her life that day. It may feel strange at first to use technology in this way. But these little reminders every day can help to foster a life of rejoicing, praying continually, and giving thanks in all circumstances.

A second action step you can take is to include structures of accountability in your life. Despite many attempts to the contrary nowadays, no one is meant to live the Christian life on his or her own. In his book *Simply Christian,* New Testament scholar N. T. Wright puts this point sharply: "it is as impossible, unnecessary, and undesirable to be a Christian all by yourself as it is to be a newborn baby all by yourself"(p. 210). Or you might consider the equally pointed words of John Wesley in his message "Upon Our Lord's Sermon on the Mount — Discourse IV": "Christianity is essentially a social religion, and . . . to turn it into a solitary religion is indeed to destroy it"(p. 195). These voices point us, in part, to the necessity of accountability in the life of a disciple of Christ. When you find that you are struggling to be attentive to general calling, the company of others who know you and who can encourage you is often just what you need. This can include both formal and informal practices. A small group that meets weekly — whether or not they have the time or feel like meeting — will develop the bonds that enable them to press each other on in the life of faith. It is also extraordinarily helpful to have people in your life who can randomly check in with aspects of your general calling: "What are you learning in Scripture lately?" "How is it going in your attempt to be patient with your sister?" "Are you still volunteering at the food bank? How are things going there?" The reality is that you will run out of steam if you try to do God's will daily on your own power. But in the power of the Holy Spirit, in the company of friends who support you, living faithfully can be a daily reality.

A third practical way forward is to focus on one specific aspect of your general calling. In the movie *What about Bob?,* there is a scene in which the therapist, Dr. Leo Marvin, encourages his patient Bob to take one small step at a time. Echoing the title of his book, Dr. Marvin tells Bob to take "baby steps" in order to manage his way through the day. Rather than thinking about all that would be required to get out of the building, for example,

Bob should think about simply getting out of that room. The cumulative weight of all of Bob's fears was addressed by isolating them and addressing them one by one. While I'm not sure if that was good therapeutic advice, it certainly applies to general calling. You will usually find that you are living more faithfully over the long haul if you begin with "baby steps." Of course, you must be careful here not to open yourself to an easy excuse to neglect certain aspects of your general calling. The standard of our shared vocation remains high, precisely because God wants the best for us and from us. But by choosing one area to work on specifically in a given week or month, you can begin to make progress toward a more comprehensive discipleship. The momentum of genuine change in one aspect in your life will propel you to focus on another area, and then another — and your life will begin to show continual fruit for God's kingdom. Over time, you will gradually become the kind of person who can sense who God made you to be. In other words, you will be in a better position for the process of discernment, which the next chapter explores.

DISCUSSION QUESTIONS

1. Do you recognize yourself in either of the two patterns described at the beginning of this chapter?

2. What people or practices in your life help to support you in living out our general calling?

3. Do you believe that living out our general calling leads to a happier life? Why or why not?

4. Which aspects of our general calling do you find most difficult to live out? Which aspects come more naturally to you?

5. Have you experienced any indicators that you might be neglecting general calling recently? If so, how can you respond?

4

How Can I Know?
The Process of Vocational Discernment

Like many first-year college students, Zach was set on changing the world. (Zach's story is used with permission.) He had spent his adolescent years living in Thailand at a home that his parents had founded. The home provided a safe alternative for girls at high risk of being co-opted into prostitution. Motivated by the effects of injustice that he saw, as well as a strong sense of the holistic nature of the gospel, he arrived at college ready to go to work. He connected with groups and events on campus addressing any number of causes: global health, clean water, literacy, poverty — the list went on. But a year or so into his college experience, something unexpected happened. He began to feel overwhelmed by the magnitude of needs in the world. On top of that, he felt pulled in too many directions. How could he make meaningful progress with such limited time and such significant needs? Ultimately, he realized that he was not the savior of the world; Jesus was the only one who could fulfill that role. Zach's life and work could serve as a sign of God's redemption of creation, by God's grace. But the weight of that redemption did not rest on Zach's shoulders.

He also came to realize something else. Looking around at the many different ways that his brothers and sisters in Christ were embodying the kingdom of God, Zach saw that each of them was using his or her unique gifts and passions. The image of the body of Christ suddenly came alive for him in a beautiful and exciting way. Once he understood that, Zach felt free to look for a particular area of focus. In the language we've been using in this book, he aimed to discern his missional calling. It took time, countless conversations, and a lot of prayer. It also required paying attention. As he did so, Zach began to notice a thread running through his life. He intentionally sought to build relationships with those who didn't appear to fit naturally into social circles, such as a young man who consistently sat alone in the dining hall. He participated in a campus ministry program aimed at exploring the complexities of homelessness and urban poverty. He was deeply moved by a chapel speaker who spoke about the pervasive concern in the Bible for those in poverty or otherwise marginalized by society. In fact, he hadn't particularly wanted to go to chapel that day, but his roommate convinced him to go at the last minute. It changed his life. Zach was finally able to piece together his missional calling: serving as a means of God's love and healing for people who feel marginalized by society. After graduating, he was able to live this out as a staff member for many years of a nonprofit ministry that serves homeless youths. He now is in his fifth year as a pastor of a congregation whose particular mission is to minister to those who feel cast out by society. While the specific means may evolve throughout his life, Zach will continue to live out his missional calling in various ways.

The process of recognizing your missional calling is the heart of vocational discernment. It is also the focus of this chapter. As you can see from Zach's story, the primary outcome of this process is not identifying a major or a career path. Rather, the main goal is to find the thread that ties together the gifts, passions, and needs that will mark your distinctive contribution to God's purposes. Once that is in place, of course, a certain academic major and career path will make more or less sense. But your missional calling is sustained throughout your entire life, and thus it will outlast any specific decision you make about an academic or career trajectory. In this light, discerning missional calling is a very specific kind of process. It is distinct from other types of discernment, such as whether to accept a job offer or try to reconcile with a former friend — though of course some of the same dynamics might be in play in these instances. You should also keep in mind that *discernment* of missional calling is not the same thing as *confirming* a case of direct calling, which we discussed in Chapter Two. Since missional calling is something that endures throughout your life, you should expect the process of identifying it to take time and attentiveness.

God made each of us with different personalities and instincts. As a former professor of mine used to say, everyone has distinct "mental furniture." In that light, different people are inclined to go about the process of discernment in varying ways. Some will be immediately drawn to rational analysis. While there is no such thing as a vocational algorithm that neatly spits out your missional calling, those who are wired to value logic might wish there were. Others will tend to follow the heart wherever it may lead. I certainly would not insist on a "one size fits all" approach to discerning missional calling, but I would suggest that it is important for both the head and the heart to play a role in the process. In her book *Hearing with the Heart*, Debra K. Farrington articulates this well: "In discernment, we strive for . . . balance between what our intellect tells us is reasonable and consistent with our understanding of the scripture's teachings about God's desires and our feelings or intuition through which we can see and hear with the heart and soul" (p. 142). As you aim to approach discernment in a manner that fits your distinct makeup, then, you are wise to consider your whole self. Enter into this process with the understanding that God can call you in a variety of ways.

Hearing that call will require clear thinking, an open heart, and careful attentiveness. Toward that end, three key practices will each play a crucial role: spiritual disciplines, self-reflection, and communal engagement.

The Role of Prayer and Other Spiritual Disciplines

Some people take an episodic approach to health and wellness. If they know they are scheduled for a physical exam in the near future, for example, such people will try to "cram" for the test. In the two or three weeks leading up to the physical, they might cut out their typical daily desserts and eat more vegetables than usual. Perhaps they engage in a rigorous exercise routine (and, unwisely, many do this without building up at a proper and moderate pace). All of this is done in the hope that the cholesterol and blood pressure screenings will not reveal clues about an unhealthy lifestyle to the doctor, to one's spouse, or even to one's conscious self. This sort of manipulation rarely fools the physician, not to mention that it also undermines the very purpose of preventative health care. The reality, of course, is that health and well-being require continual attention. The purpose of screenings is to indicate when there is a need to adjust one's daily habits. If someone is not making good choices on a consistent basis, then it doesn't really matter what the results of a physical exam might be. It will make little difference in one's overall life.

In a similar way, you may try to take an episodic approach to vocational discernment. Faced with questions about yourself and choices to make about the future, you may turn to practices that are not normally part of your life. Rambling your way through awkward prayers, or puzzling over the pages of a crisp and unused Bible, you may try your hand at the sorts of things that people turn to with questions about calling. But discernment best arises out of a continual commitment to knowing God more deeply rather than from an occasional approach. This is not to say that you shouldn't practice the spiritual disciplines if you don't have a lot of experience with them. You have to start somewhere. What I am saying is that you must recognize that the purpose of the spiritual disciplines is not to answer your questions — it's to be drawn more deeply into the love and knowledge of God. First things must come first. If you set your heart and mind on connecting with God, the spiritual disciplines are one of the means by which you will be transformed. As you do so, you will come to learn the sound of God's voice. This is the process by which vocational discernment becomes possible. On the other hand, approaching these practices merely as a means of helping you make vocational choices will likely make little long-term impact on your life.

There is no official or formal list of spiritual disciplines in the Christian tradition. Still, a variety of practices have deep grounding in the church's heritage and continue to shape Christian lives. Of those, I want to consider four in particular: prayer, reading Scripture, fasting, and giving. While I want to be very clear that these are not the only spiritual disciplines that relate to vocational discernment, all four of them have their place in that process. As you explore these practices, keep in mind an idea that we examined in Chapter Two. The spiritual disciplines are not a method of transforming yourself, nor are they a way of guaranteeing a particular result. In them you are coming before a living God who is not accountable to your demands or your sense of timing. Instead, these practices are a way of creating space in your life for God to work. They get you in the habit of waiting for God actively, humbly, and expectantly.

Commitment to regular prayer is a fundamental way of making that kind of space. It is quite clear that a prayerful life is a key part of every Christian's general calling. Yet cultivating the habit of prayer is also essential to the process of discerning missional calling. You can think of missional calling as the primary point of connection between God's redemptive work in the world and the particularity of each person. In that light, discovering that point of connection will require the time and effort to know God and to know yourself. That, precisely, is the work of prayer. And the way in which you approach this work makes a significant difference when it comes to discernment. I want to suggest that your missional calling will emerge more naturally if your prayer life is marked by three specific traits: attentiveness, honesty, and discipline.

Attentiveness is, in many ways, the heart of prayer. Stop, quiet your soul, and take notice. Give praise as you reflect on God's nature and attributes. Give thanks for the specific ways God has blessed you. Lift up the needs that are revealed when you pay attention to your life and the lives of others. Ask forgiveness as your heart and mind recount the ways in which you've fallen short. Simply rest in God's comforting presence. As you do these things — that is, as you pay attention — you cannot help coming to a deeper knowledge of both God and yourself. Again, I want to emphasize that this is not a quick and easy path to vocational discernment. Rather, a pattern of attentiveness to God and to your life over the long haul is necessary to preparing the ground through which your missional calling can emerge.

True attentiveness is possible only if you also approach prayer in complete honesty. People are often tempted to hold back their true selves when they approach God in prayer. Whether out of guilt, or fear, or theological assumptions that are just plain wrong, some people want to present a sanitized version of themselves in prayer. The problem is that when you hold your true self back from God, you are not opening yourself to the very One who can heal those parts of you that you may feel need to be hidden. The Psalms provide a wonderful model for genuine prayer, with their dizzying variety of deep mourning, heartfelt anger, and exuberant praise. As April Yamasaki, in her book *Sacred Pauses*, suggests about the people who wrote the Psalms, "theirs were not always nice prayers, not always 'proper' prayers, not always prayers that I would feel comfortable praying, but they were honest prayers that revealed the depth of their relationship with God" (p. 57). I've long thought that the very inclusion of the Psalms in the canon of Scripture was a way of signaling to God's people that raw and unedited prayers are not only acceptable, they are in fact necessary. God is fully up to the task of working with us as we are.

Of course, attentiveness and honesty can go only so far in a sporadic prayer life. Prayer is called a spiritual discipline precisely because discipline is essential to the practice. I must quickly add that discipline in this context does not mean punishing yourself harshly if you miss a prayer time. Rather, discipline here means *commitment*. It refers to making prayer a regular, habitual part of your life. Unfortunately, prayer too often gets relegated to the corners of life that are left over after other priorities have collected their dues. Or, perhaps you turn to prayer only when you feel like it. But prayer that is dependent on the mercy of a busy schedule or the whims of emotion is not likely to cultivate the soil for genuine spiritual formation. True knowledge of God and yourself becomes possible when you commit to making space for God in hurried times as well as times of leisure, whether or not you may feel like it. The really good news here is that once you begin to make that sort of disciplined prayer part of your life, it becomes more natural to keep it up — just like with any discipline. When you grow accustomed to connecting with God in the deep places of your soul, you long for more. What begins as a discipline becomes as normal as eating and sleeping. It is in precisely that context of attentive, honest, and habitual prayer that you are enabled to see yourself in all your uniqueness, which is the very stuff of discerning missional calling.

Along with prayer, immersing yourself in Scripture is a key practice that shapes you for discernment. People read the Bible for all sorts of reasons. Some look for historical data or literary inspiration, while others search for ethical guidance. But to read the Bible as a spiritual discipline is to read it as a means of encountering God and being formed by God through that encounter. A great deal has been written about reading Scripture as a spiritual discipline. (Eugene H. Peterson's *Eat This Book: A Conversation in the Art of Spiritual Reading* is an excellent place to start.) The concern here has to do specifically with the relationship between that practice and the discernment of missional calling. The point is not to read the Bible with the hopes of finding a particular passage that articulates your missional calling (though of course there is no reason to rule out the possibility that a specific portion of the Bible will play a role in the process). Rather, the aim is to be transformed by God in and through your attentiveness to the fullness of God's word. People who dwell in Scripture know who they are. They see the relentlessness with which God has called creation back to God's self. They taste the joy of responding to that call by grace. They hear the commission to live as active signs of the reconciling work of God. When your senses are engaged by this kind of meditation on Scripture, you are able to begin to recognize the specific role that you might play in that broader story.

And what *kind* of reading, you might ask, enables that sort of response? After all, plenty of people have struggled and strained to make sense of a particular passage from Deuteronomy or Jude only to encounter frustration. The trouble often occurs when you try to read your way to God rather than waiting in the text for God to work in you. Like any spiritual discipline, reading Scripture is a way of creating space for God rather than a means of forcing God to action. In that regard, the way forward is to open your whole self to God prayerfully, humbly, and patiently as you engage the biblical text. This is true even when you encounter challenging or puzzling passages. As with prayer, making a habit of immersing yourself in God's word regularly enables genuine formation over the long haul. Often, a good way to foster this kind of prayerful reading is to engage a text of a manageable size. I often encourage students to read "shorter and deeper," meaning reading smaller chunks of texts more attentively and expectantly. Sometimes, you may have little sense that anything much has happened or changed in you. But eventually, with patience, God's "living and active" word (Heb. 4:12) will begin to do its work in you. As the theologian Origen of Alexandria wrote in the third century, your mind and feelings are "touched by a divine breath" as you ponder the Bible reverently. While you can't force that kind of an experience to happen, you can think of the practice of reading Scripture as an active way of waiting for it. Those who commit to spending time with God's word in expectant hope for God's Spirit to move are in a good posture for discernment.

Fasting is a spiritual discipline that has fallen off of the radar screen in many corners of the church. The practice of fasting involves refraining from eating food for a short period of time to focus on prayer and self-examination. It has a long and deep history in the Christian tradition. And yet many Christians rarely hear anything about it nowadays, perhaps because of concerns about excessive self-denial or suspicion about outward works. While such concerns are understandable, there is great potential in this discipline if approached carefully and thoughtfully. It is wise to seek appropriate pastoral and medical advice before practicing fasting for the first time. It is also worth keeping in mind Jesus' advice about fasting in Matthew 6:16-18; namely, that the point is not to put on a display of piety for others to see but to focus on God. Fasting for just one meal, for example, can be an illuminating and formative practice. Particularly in the process of discernment, focusing on God through fasting can reveal dimensions of yourself that you might not otherwise see. Richard J. Foster, in his book *Celebration of Discipline*, describes this sort of experience vividly: "More than any other discipline, fasting reveals the things that control us . . . We cover up what is inside us with food and other good things, but in fasting these things surface. . . . Anger, bitterness, jealousy, strife, fear — if they are within us, they will surface during fasting" (p. 55). As you begin to recognize the things that may have been interfering with your formation in the likeness of Christ, you can welcome God's work in clearing them away. As that happens, you may begin to see layers within yourself that you had not previously been able to see. Missional calling can begin to show itself as you gain a fresh and honest view of who you are.

The spiritual discipline of giving refers to offering time, money, and things to God by way of one's neighbor. The most obvious expression of this discipline is the practice of tithing, or giving a tenth of one's income to one's local congregation. But it can and should take other expressions as well. Volunteering as a tutor, organizing a diaper drive for a local food and clothing bank, offering professional expertise to a local advocacy organization — the possibilities are almost endless. Sometimes you may not think of practicing such acts of service as a spiritual discipline. But that's precisely what it can be, especially when approached in terms of making room in your life for God to work in transformative ways. At its heart, the discipline of giving is about God's work of orienting your priorities rightly. It functions both as a signal and as a catalyst. The regular practice of giving functions as a signal by showing you where your priorities really are. If you pay attention, you will begin to identify those areas where you are prone to hold back from offering everything back to God. "For where your treasure is," Jesus said in Luke 12:34, "there your heart will be also." If you find it relatively easy to tithe and give financially but wince at the thought of offering your time, then you have an indicator of a schedule that is in danger of becoming an idol in your life. Alternately, perhaps someone is perfectly happy to serve weekly in any number of capacities at church and in the community but struggles to let go of money or possessions. It is worth considering that this may be a sign of holding on to the wrong things. Just as fasting can uncover damaging spiritual patterns, so also can regular giving reveal misaligned priorities.

Giving can also function as a catalyst. By making a commitment to give even in those areas that are particularly difficult, you open yourself to a new possibility. That is, you welcome the work of God in realigning your priorities through the very acts of giving. As I've said repeatedly with these disciplines, this is not an automatic process. But a habit of intentional giving makes for very fertile ground in the work of transformation. When this change begins to happen, your sense of missional calling can become clearer as well. Recall Zach's story from the beginning of the chapter. Rather than trying to give to every worthy need in the world, he came to recognize a particular heart for one need. He found that he could respond to that need in a variety of ways. You also might identify a particular need that orients your giving — perhaps it's homelessness, or global health, or youth ministry, or food insecurity. If you do find a specific need that calls out to you, it's a great practice to commit to some sort of regular giving. Generally, when people wait until they think they have enough time or financial stability to give, they never get around to it. The thing to remember is that the amount of giving does not matter as much as the commitment to give consistently in all three areas (time, money, and possessions). You will likely find that the practice of this spiritual discipline helps you both to discern and to begin to live out your missional calling.

The Role of Self-Reflection

The role that the spiritual disciplines play in the process of vocational discernment is somewhat different from the role played by the next two categories. This is because the spiritual disciplines are not initiated for the sake of that process, but they prepare the ground to make discernment possible. And, of course, the spiritual disciplines remain important long after someone has identified his or her missional calling. So even though it is unwise (and perhaps impossible) to discern missional calling without engaging those practices, they have a larger role in life than enabling vocational discernment. The next two practices that we'll explore, vocational self-examination and communal discernment, are more specifically directed toward the goal of identifying missional calling. While you might engage in self-reflection or participate in community in any number of ways throughout your life, what I have in mind here are very specific forms of those practices. To begin, consider what is involved in the practice of looking deep into your life for signs of a missional calling.

It is crucial that the process of vocational self-reflection is *intentional*. While we have seen that a person does not need to go looking for direct or general calling, missional calling is something that you really do need to seek out. Rarely will someone's specific contribution to God's kingdom simply appear out of thin air. It's important to be honest with yourself that you're looking for your missional calling. The very consciousness that you have begun a discernment process can nudge you to look in corners of your life that you might not otherwise explore. And quite apart from the purpose of discernment, such explorations can increase your love and wonder for the uniqueness of each of God's creatures — including you.

This process can start in different places. For example, I usually describe the idea of missional calling early on in my first-year student seminar on vocation. Then I ask the students how much they know of their calling at that point in their lives. A few already have a well-developed sense of what they would like their contribution to be. A few have no idea at all, or at least they haven't considered what unique gifts and passions they have to offer. Most students usually have some idea but not yet a complete picture of their missional calling. "I know it has something to do with children," one might say; or for another, "I want to use my love of words somehow." Wherever you are, you can begin this process with a very specific goal. At the end of the process, you want to be able to articulate your missional calling in a sentence or two. It may take a matter of months to get to that point, or it may take a few years. But you won't likely get there if you don't begin the journey.

It's also important to know just what your self-reflection should focus on in order to help reveal your missional calling. Essentially, there are three objectives: recognizing what you're good at, finding your passions, and identifying the need that you are most compelled to address. The first objective takes for granted that God has endowed each person with unique gifts. These gifts help you both to recognize and to fulfill your missional calling. You are wise to think as broadly as you can about this first goal. This would include spiritual gifts such as prophecy, ministry, teaching, exhortation, giving, leadership, or compassion, to draw from the list used in Romans 12:6-8. It would also include such natural abilities as facility with numbers, a knack for designing and understanding complex systems, or a way with words. All of these come from God, and all of them can be utilized in a missional calling. A very natural first step in a process of vocational self-examination, then, is to consider carefully where you are gifted.

There is no set formula for self-reflection on gifts, but there are plenty of ways to get started. A very interesting exercise is simply to write down three things that you do well. Rather than dwelling on this exercise for too long, it's best to write down a few abilities or gifts that come immediately to mind. Then think back over your life. Over your years in school, what areas came naturally to you and where did you earn your strongest grades? Where have other people consistently given you compliments or affirmation? This is especially helpful when you've received similar compliments from different people in a variety of contexts. What qualities or traits do you value in yourself the most? What qualities or traits have others said they value in you? At this stage, your focus is not necessarily on what you love, but what you do well. So if you find a strong ability in math or a gift for leadership coming up again and again, write that down even if you don't feel particularly drawn to it. Ideally, you're looking for areas of overlap between what you have seen in yourself and what others have noticed. After some reflection, look back at the initial three items that you wrote down. Were those affirmed by thinking back over your life, or does your initial list need some adjusting? Do you need to add to or subtract from the list? Either way, this exercise is not the end of the discernment process. It's a starting point to take prayerfully and observantly into the coming months or years. As your discernment process continues, watch to see if that list of gifts is affirmed or refined by further reflection.

It is also very helpful to identify those areas that will never be strengths for you. What do you know you're *not* created to do? All of us struggle and fail at certain times in our lives. Repeated difficulties in a specific area can be a sign that you have simply found one of your limits. While this can be disappointing, sometimes excruciatingly so, discovering a limit is actually a blessing in vocational discernment. As Parker J. Palmer suggests in *Let Your Life Speak,* "each of us arrives here with a nature, which means both limits and potentials. We can learn as much about our nature by running into our limits as by experiencing our potentials" (pp. 41-42). Once you know that something is clearly not part of your missional calling, you can look in other places to find your strengths. Of course, not every difficulty is a sign of a true limit. Sometimes you can fail because you don't prepare well, or because you give up too easily, or because you are distracted by something else. The key is learning to identify when a failure is a sign of something you really cannot do and when it is instead a sign of a challenge that you need to press through or approach differently. This leads to one of the most important skills of vocational discernment: the ability to distinguish between a *genuine limit* and a *temporary setback.*

When something lies beyond your capacity no matter how hard you try, then you have come upon a genuine limit. Some people just don't have it in them to master quantum physics. Others may never be able to develop the patience needed for a missional calling involving young children. Those who are strongly extroverted cannot simply make themselves comfortable working in solitude for extended periods of time. True, sometimes your limits lie far beyond where you initially expect them to be. But everyone still has limits, and they should instruct you in discerning your missional calling. A temporary setback, on the other hand, refers to a challenge that you are able to press through as you live out your missional calling. Any worthwhile purpose in life will bring times of struggle and difficulty. Some competencies come very naturally to you, but others are developed only out of tremendous effort and persistence. A temporary setback may be a failure, a time of discomfort, or an initial mediocre performance. But over time and with sufficient work, you can move past a temporary setback.

How, then, can you tell the difference between them? After all, most of us can look back on a temporary setback that felt at the time like it was a genuine limit. If you acknowledge that something is a limit, aren't you potentially giving up too early? These are really good questions, and they are crucial ones to ask in discernment. Three things need to be said in response. First, watch for improvement over time. One failure should not be taken as an indicator of a genuine limit. But if you persist in trying to develop a capacity and improvement is just not visible over time, then that is a sign of a limit. Second, make sure that you have addressed everything that is under your control. For example, difficulties that result from poor preparation do not suggest a genuine limit; they suggest a lack of effort. Third, do not confuse God's power with God's calling. What I mean is that some people willfully ignore genuine limits because of their (very appropriate) belief that God is all-powerful. Those inclined to this kind of move often cite, somewhat out of context, Philippians 4:13: "I can do all things through him who strengthens me." The idea is that no limit is insurmountable if you exert enough effort, because God is able to do anything. But the problem is that God's *ability* to do anything does not mean that God *will* do whatever you want. I believe that God is able to give me a 95-mile-per-hour fastball or make me sing like an angel — but anyone who has seen me pitch or heard me sing will confirm that God has not chosen to do so. In other words, you need to keep in mind the difference between direct calling and missional calling. Where God gives a clear calling to a particular task, then God will fully equip you to do it. But when you're trying to discern missional calling, one way in which God can guide you to your goal is by showing you where your limits lie.

Let's consider an example. Suppose a second-year college student has long thought that his missional calling involves caring for people's health, and his dream is to live this out professionally as a doctor. He takes organic chemistry, a required pre-med course, and struggles mightily. When his grades are posted, his heart drops when he sees a D. Should he take this as a sign of a genuine limit? The best answer is "not yet," but he should pay close attention. Suppose he takes the course a second time, putting in even more time and effort in his daily studies. Whereas he struggled through a bout of the flu the first time through the course, he remains healthy the second time. He uses a study group, which he didn't do the first time. If he does all of these things and gets a B, then that is a solid indicator that he is dealing with a temporary setback. However, if he makes all of those changes and gets a D+, then it is time to consider seriously that he may be bumping up against a genuine limit. Like most aspects of vocational discernment, differentiating between limits and setbacks is not an exact science. But persistence and watching for improvement will usually give you a good indicator of how you might move forward.

Along with looking for your gifts, a process of vocational self-reflection should also involve exploring what you love. Many Christians are terrified of the notion of God's calling because they are sure that God will ask them to commit their lives to something they dread. While I can't promise that you will never receive a direct calling that leads you beyond your comfort zone, there is very good news when it comes to missional calling. God gave you certain passions to be used. Your missional calling is a long-term pattern of how you will participate in God's reconciling work, and it aligns with the unique way in which God created you. That includes your loves. I'm not referring here to those activities that you merely enjoy. Riding a roller coaster or playing a video game may give you a feeling of pleasure, but a passion runs deeper. A passion is something that gives you a sense of fulfillment, a sense of contribution. It is something that can be used to "build up the body of Christ," to borrow the language of Ephesians 4:12. In the process, it gives you the sense of living into the purpose for which you were made. A passion might be writing, gathering groups of people together for conversation, teaching, seeing people experience God's love for the first time, helping others find their gifts, or taking on unseen acts of service, to name just a few. The list of possibilities goes on and on.

Some people can identify their passions immediately, but for others it will take some time and thought. What are your deepest moments of joy in life? What are some experiences in the last few years that made you feel more alive? When have you felt the rush of a job well done? Just as with identifying your gifts, it's a good idea to begin writing down the ideas that come to mind. If you are having trouble identifying any passions, you're not alone. Many students have told me over the years that they have trouble finding anything that gets them particularly motivated. Quite often, the issue is that they simply have not tried enough new experiences to find a passion that may be lurking within. (I certainly do not want to dismiss the possibility that there may be emotional or physiological dynamics involved in such cases. If you feel that might be true for you, I would encourage you to seek a referral for a good counselor from someone you trust.) If you find it difficult to articulate any deep loves, it may be a good idea to try something new. Volunteer in a brand new area of service in your church. Take a class in an area that you have never considered before. Offer your services to a local non-profit organization. Find an opportunity to speak in front of a group. Not only will these options expand your circle of experience, but they also help to shift your focus off yourself. Somewhat paradoxically, you can often discover your deepest passions precisely when your attention is directed on others. This leads very naturally to the third objective of vocational self-reflection, which is to identify the primary need in the world that you are called to address.

Not only is it important that your missional calling make use of your gifts and passions, but those gifts and passions should also be directed toward a specific goal. Merely wanting "to write" is not yet a missional calling, but writing to achieve a particular purpose may well be. Desiring "to help people" is too general to be a missional calling — in what specific way do you want to help people? In other words, your missional calling identifies a need that you are particularly suited to address. This is not to limit the ways in which God might use you; rather, the purpose is to sharpen your own focus. General calling would suggest that each of you will find places of service both within and beyond the local church, and there will be considerable variety in the ways you serve over the course of a lifetime. But when a particular need grabs your heart, you will continually look for new ways to address that need throughout your life. That sustained pattern of contribution is precisely what a missional calling articulates.

While meeting a need just for the sake of meeting a need would be worthwhile, you should also keep in mind the broader perspective of God's purposes. Striving to reduce food insecurity, for example, does not only hold the potential to make lives better. It also can serve as a sign of God's reconciling of all creation. The very idea of a missional calling presumes that your efforts can point to God's kingdom, at least as a foretaste. In that light, the diverse ways that God's people choose to focus their lives all have parts to play. Some will be focused more directly on the community of faith, while others will sense a missional calling oriented to the world as a whole. God's purposes are vast; in fact, Colossians 1:20 suggests that they are nothing less than reconciling all things to God. While that is ultimately God's work and not ours, we get a glimpse of that reconciliation when someone makes clean water available to a new community. We get a glimpse when someone else teaches a group of third-graders at a local church with passion and enthusiasm. We get a glimpse when someone else negotiates a peaceful solution to a volatile political crisis. What need has taken hold of your heart? What do you hope is included in the first paragraph of your obituary (even if you hope it is written a long time from now)? If you find some connection between that need, your passions, and your gifts, then you are well on your way to identifying your missional calling.

The Role of Communal Discernment

Even if your process of vocational self-reflection has generated a sense of a missional calling that seems to fit you, your work of discernment is not finished. Just as all are designed to mature as Christians in the context of community, so also you come to know yourself better through interaction with other people. To move forward with a sense of missional calling without involving others in discernment is usually a mistake. Those who know you best have a perspective on your life that you may not initially be able to see. This does not for a moment mean that someone else should take over the process of discerning your missional calling. In fact, you should regard with caution anyone who claims assertively to know exactly what God has in store for you. You are ultimately responsible for hearing and responding to God's call on your life. But the process of hearing well entails listening to the insights that others have to offer. This is true no matter what your process of vocational self-reflection might have generated.

When thinking about the people you wish to involve in discerning missional calling, variety is key. Think in terms of people who have known you for a long time as well as those who are deeply involved in your life now. Those who have known you longest, such as parents, siblings, and childhood friends, can remind you especially of what you were like early in your life. Sometimes a conversation like this can remind you of a childhood love or tendency that the intervening years have slowly faded. Yet there is also real value in the perspectives of those who may not have known you for a long time but interact with you on a regular basis. Passions or abilities that you have discovered in recent years might be evident to those who are part of your daily life now (and perhaps not as evident to those who still see you through the lens of who you might have been in the past). College students in particular often note how quickly deep friendships can form in the context of campus life. Without a doubt there is value for discernment in lifelong relationships, but there is also insight to be gleaned from newer ones.

It is also a good idea to seek out both individuals and a small group in the process of communal discernment. Invite someone to a one-on-one conversation over coffee, and let that person know right up front why you want to meet. I suspect you'll find that most people are more than willing to be involved in your vocational exploration. After a few of these conversations, pay attention to how much variation there is in the feedback you're receiving. Do the people you're talking with perceive the same gifts and loves in you? Are there sharp differences among them? Once you've spoken with a number of individuals, invite some people together for a group conversation. (Or, if you're already part of a regular small group, ask if one of your sessions can focus on vocational discernment.) The interaction between people who know you well can provide a new level of insight, particularly if you are willing to listen patiently as the conversation develops. If you received a number of different responses in one-on-one conversations, then include some of those same people in the group discussion. If there was a lot of consistency among individual perspectives, then consider inviting new people to the small group. It may feel a bit strange at first to ask people to participate in that kind of a conversation. But once you muster the courage, you will usually find that people are honored to play such a significant role in your life. In fact, you may inspire some of them to consider their own vocation more intentionally.

In either a one-on-one or a group conversation around discernment, it is usually best to begin with open-ended questions. You might consider some of the following: How would you describe my personality? What do you see as some of my gifts? When have I appeared most joyful and fulfilled? What kinds of contributions could you see me making to God's kingdom? If your vocational self-reflection generated a one- or two-sentence statement of missional calling, it's best to hold that aside at first. You can wait until you've heard the responses from others, and asked any appropriate follow-up questions, before sharing what you discovered in your self-reflection. When you do finally share your own perspective, then the conversation can explore the similarities and differences among what was shared. Sometimes this kind of a conversation will strongly confirm what emerged from self-reflection. In other cases, a different sense of missional calling will develop in and through the conversation with others. Often it will be some combination of the two. No matter what transpires, the interaction is very worthwhile. By inviting trusted others into your process, you are opening yourself to the variety of ways in which God can guide you into the future.

Taking Action

The idea of beginning a process of self-reflection and communal discernment, rooted in the good soil of a long-term commitment to the spiritual disciplines, might seem daunting. But if you have not yet identified your missional calling, then discernment itself might be your immediate vocation. Thinking in these terms offers two advantages. First, it reminds you that discovering missional calling is not quick and easy, and thus you will be more inclined to commit time and energy to the process. Second, it highlights the importance of channeling your abilities and loves in a particular and worthy direction. True, there is no doubt that God can use you in many ways before you have identified your missional calling. Yet that realization does not minimize the importance of seeking out the distinctive fingerprint of your life's purpose.

Committing yourself to taking action is the best way to avoid the pitfall of *vocational inertia.* In physics, the principle of inertia refers to the tendency of physical objects to remain in their current state. Objects at rest tend to remain at rest, and objects in motion tend to remain in motion. That principle presents a nice image of what can happen in your own life with respect to vocational discernment. Many people are comfortable with the idea that, at some point down the road, they will figure out where their lives are going. They know that they want a sense of what their unique contribution will be, but for now it seems out of reach. Perhaps this is because they believe it will fall out of the sky at some point in the future, or perhaps it is because they are afraid of what they might find. So they wait. And people vocationally at rest tend to remain at rest. Of course, the principle of inertia can also work for you rather than against you. Once you take a step of discernment — writing down some gifts, perhaps, or talking with a parent — the next step becomes easier. Momentum is built up, and the process now in motion tends to continue.

As important as it is for vocational discernment to begin, it cannot continue indefinitely. You certainly do not want to rush the slow, deliberate work of discernment. But neither do you want to prolong it without end. In any discernment process, you run the danger of *vocational wandering*. This refers to a never-ending pattern of seeking your missional calling, which ultimately prevents you from actually living it out. Whether after months or years, the time eventually comes to take what you've learned and move forward. Those who tend to be perfectionists are particularly inclined to vocational wandering, since they want to be absolutely sure that they've got it right before bringing the process to a close. But here is the point to remember: concluding your time of discernment does not mean that your formulation of missional calling is absolutely fixed. It can and likely will be revised as life goes on. Your missional calling tends to endure throughout your life, but the way that you articulate it might be refined through new experiences. You will find new contexts in which to live it out, and perhaps you will even find further gifts, loves, or needs to incorporate into it. After prayerful self-reflection and communal discernment, then, take your sentence or two and go with it. The wording isn't set in stone. But the God who made you and called you is faithful. So you can walk forward in confidence and with direction, offering what you have to God's creative and redemptive hand. With that in mind, the final chapter will consider what these ideas about vocation might mean for your understanding of God.

DISCUSSION QUESTIONS

1. To what extent do you know your missional calling at this point in your life? Are you aware of at least some of the elements of it?

2. Which of the spiritual disciplines described in this chapter are currently part of your life? Which ones would you like to begin practicing regularly?

3. Try to think of an experience in your life that really energized you or made you feel most alive. Does that experience tell you anything about your gifts, your passions, or the need in the world that you feel most compelled to address?

4. Have you ever identified a genuine limit or something that will just never be a strength for you? Does knowing this help you in discerning your missional calling?

5. Who are some of the people you would invite to participate in a process of discernment with you? Why would you choose them?

5

Who Is Calling?
Getting Your Theological Bearings

I love a good baseball movie, and my favorite is *Field of Dreams*. In that 1989 film, Kevin Costner plays an Iowa farmer named Ray Kinsella. While working in his cornfield one day, Ray hears a voice call out in a gravelly whisper, "If you build it, he will come." He also sees an accompanying vision of a baseball field and a lone baseball player standing on it. Without knowing for sure *how* he knows, Ray is convinced that the voice is guiding him to plow under his corn and build a baseball field on his property. If he does so, he believes, the great left fielder "Shoeless" Joe Jackson will somehow come back to life and play on the field. Despite gossiping neighbors and the dictates of financial prudence — corn is the source of his family's income, after all — Ray builds the field. Eventually, the ghost (or something like it) of Shoeless Joe Jackson does indeed come to play baseball on the field.

After such an unusual turn of events, Ray might reasonably expect that the voice would leave him alone. Instead, it leads him on a new series of odd and unexpected adventures. The next message Ray hears, "ease his pain," leads him to drive to Boston to take a reclusive writer to Fenway Park to watch a baseball game. At the game, Ray hears the voice instructing him to "go the distance." He and the writer, who also heard the voice and saw the corresponding vision, determine that they should go a small town in

Minnesota to look for an obscure baseball player-turned-doctor. Eventually their journey leads them back to the Kinsella farm in Iowa, where the spirits of many old-time baseball players are playing the game they love once again.

Throughout this strange adventure, Ray is remarkably obedient to whoever or whatever is calling him to each new step. Alternately referring to the source as "the voice" or "the universe," Ray does what he is told (with the support of a stunningly patient wife through it all). One of the most interesting exchanges in the film occurs near the end, as the players are wrapping up a day of enjoying their beloved pastime. Shoeless Joe repeats the words of the first calling to Ray: "If you build it, he will come." As he says this, Joe points to a player who is taking off his catcher's mask. When the player's face is revealed, Ray sees that it is the spirit of his late father. With a look of realization on his face, Ray repeats the other messages to himself: "Ease his pain; go the distance." Believing he now knows the identity of the voice that has been calling him, he turns back towards Shoeless Joe. "It was you," Ray whispers. Quietly correcting him, Joe responds: "No, Ray, it was you."

One of the reasons that this movie remains so compelling to me is what it suggests about vocation. For Ray Kinsella, the journey was not only about being obedient to the one calling him. It was about coming to *know* the one calling him, and that was only possible by taking the journey. A significant part of what was driving Ray was the need to discover the identity of the voice. By the end, he realized that his calling came from his deepest self — the mixture of longing and regret that needed some sort of resolution. In contrast to what Ray experienced, of course, your vocation does not ultimately come from inside yourself. Calling in all its forms — general, missional, and direct — comes from God. But where Ray's story may resonate with yours is in the discovery that obedience leads to greater knowledge of the one calling. As the contours of your vocation take shape in your life, you will come to a deeper sense of the God who is their source. Ultimately, God's calling is not as much about what God wants you to do as it is about knowing and loving God.

Any understanding of vocation implies a particular vision of the God who calls you. This chapter considers the theological dimensions of the portrait of vocation that has been drawn in this book. Reflections are no substitute, of course, for actually taking the journey. As Ray Kinsella found, truly recognizing the voice of the caller requires responding to the call. Still, for Christians, the journey of vocation is taken in the company of others who have helped to point the way. The witness of generations of fellow travelers in the Christian tradition gives a picture of what you might expect to find along the path. In his book *Mere Christianity*, C. S. Lewis uses an analogy to make this point vividly. "Doctrines are not God: they are only a kind of map. But that map is based on the experience of hundreds of people who really were in touch with God — experiences compared with which any thrills or pious feelings you and I are likely to get on our own are very elementary and very confused. And secondly, if you want to get any further, you must use the map" (p. 136). Christian doctrine is no substitute for experiencing God directly, but at its best it does point the way to such direct experience. In the reflections that follow, we will explore four areas of theological terrain: the tension of God's nearness and otherness, the doctrine of the Trinity, the relationship between divine and human agency, and worship.

God's Immanence and Transcendence

The Orthodox theologian Kallistos Ware offers a striking observation in his book *The Orthodox Way:* "The traveler upon the spiritual

Way, the further he advances, becomes increasingly conscious of two contrasting facts — of the *otherness* and yet the *nearness* of the Eternal" (p. 11). Ware does not suggest that a person's sense of one of these attributes decreases as the other increases. Rather, he contends that the deeper you go into the Christian life, the more you are aware of both realities. As you become more attuned to God's presence and activity in your life, you simultaneously perceive the depth of God's mystery. We have experience with something similar to this even in finite human relationships. Spouses, for example, will often find that the more they get to know each other — even after many years together — the more they realize how much there is yet to know. But what you find in human relationships is only a pale analogy to your experience of an infinite God. The term "transcendence" is often used to convey the sense of God's otherness, while the term "immanence" aims to capture the nearness of God. The essential tension between them is at the heart of the Christian vision of God. Subordinating either reality can distort your experience of the Christian life, including your sense of calling.

It is important to get a clear sense of what is meant by each claim. When some Christians think about God's transcendence, their minds tend to focus on spatial relationships. They assume that it means that God is "out there" somewhere, far beyond the world in which we live. But this sort of understanding of transcendence is misleading in two respects. First, thinking in such terms tends to render God as just another finite object in the universe — a uniquely capable one, to be sure, but finite nonetheless. Children sometimes wonder if, with a powerful enough spacecraft, one could travel far enough through space to reach God. Adults might tend to chuckle at such memories, and yet for some the idea of transcendence as a great distance seems to persist stubbornly. A second problem is that a spatial conception of transcendence might undermine the very practical purpose of affirming God's otherness: to keep us from supposing that we have God figured out. By assuming that mere distance keeps us from seeing the fullness of God, we miss the fundamental difference between God and everything else.

At its heart, the claim of God's transcendence is not about distance. It's about mystery. It points to something about God and to something about us. A transcendent God is not one thing among many in the universe. We are moving in the right direction, in fact, if we shift our thinking around to consider the universe and everything in it to depend on God at every moment for its existence. While God is present to every dimension of the universe, nothing in our experience captures or contains the full reality of God. Scripture abounds with reminders of God's transcendence. Consider Isaiah 55:8-9:

> For my thoughts are not your thoughts,
>> nor are your ways my ways, says the Lord.
> For as the heavens are higher than the earth,
>> so are my ways higher than your ways
>> and my thoughts higher than your thoughts.

In Romans 11:33-36, the apostle Paul's affirmation of God's transcendence turns naturally to praise:

> O the depth of the riches and wisdom and knowledge of God! How unsearchable are his judgments and how inscrutable his ways!

> "For who has known the mind of the Lord?
>> Or who has been his counselor?"
> "Or who has given a gift to him,
>> to receive a gift in return?"

For from him and through him and to him are all things. To
him be the glory forever. Amen.

For us, in fact, affirming God's transcendence is an important
spiritual practice. It offers an ongoing check against pride, reminding us to resist the temptation to believe we are able fully
to comprehend God. It also helps to guard against idolatry, for
the moment we think we have God fully contained in our understanding is the moment that we turn to a false God. Worship
of the true God requires that we leave space for what we are not
capable of taking in.

Of course, the recognition that God is transcendent does not
for a moment mean that we worship an empty, mysterious void.
Nor does it mean that God is primarily a concept or an idea. The
Christian tradition has insisted that God is immanent; that God
is intimately involved in our lives and present to all of creation.
As we read in Psalm 139:7-10:

> Where can I go from your spirit?
>> Or where can I flee from your presence?
> If I ascend to heaven, you are there;
>> if I make my bed in Sheol, you are there.
> If I take the wings of the morning
>> and settle at the farthest limits of the sea,
> even there your hand shall lead me,
>> and your right hand shall hold me fast.

When Paul addressed the Athenians in Acts 17, he proclaimed
that in God "we live and move and have our being" (v. 28). To
affirm God's immanence is not just to recognize God's presence
throughout the world; it is also to affirm God's involvement with
the details of our lives. As Rowan Williams puts it in *Tokens of*

Trust, "there is nowhere God is absent, powerless, or irrelevant; no situation in the universe in the face of which God is at a loss. Which is much the same as saying that there is no situation in which God is not to be relied upon" (p. 16). Keeping this in mind will help ward off the notion that God created the world and then left it to its own devices. On the contrary, God remains relationally present to every inch of creation.

God's immanence also means that God can be known, at least in the manner and to the degree that the divine self-disclosure has made possible for finite human beings. In other words, recognizing God's transcendence protects us from the folly of supposing we understand God completely, and recognizing God's immanence prevents the despair of imagining we don't know God at all. In his memoir *Now and Then,* Frederick Buechner describes the process by which he was gradually drawn to Christ: "Though I was brought up in a family where church played virtually no role at all, through a series of events from childhood on I was moved, for the most part without any inkling of it, closer and closer to a feeling for that Mystery out of which the church arose in the first place until, finally, the Mystery itself came to have a face for me, and the face it came to have for me was the face of Christ" (p. 4). Buechner does not suggest that the mystery was eliminated when he came to perceive it expressed in Christ. Rather, his point seems to be that God's self-revelation in an actual body in time and space — that of Jesus — provides a uniquely clear vision of God for finite creatures. Rather than diminishing our sense of God's transcendence, that vision heightens it as we apprehend the lengths God has gone to in order to reach us.

You may wonder at this point what any of this has to do with vocation. There are at least three reasons why both God's immanence and God's transcendence matter greatly for framing your understanding of calling. First, you can recognize a missional or direct calling to be genuinely from God without supposing you now have God figured out. As you respond obediently to that calling, you often come to an even stronger sense of it than when you first received it. And yet, as Ware suggested, you will simultaneously grow more aware of God's otherness and mystery. It is important to keep this in mind in perceiving and acting on a particular vocation, as there will sometimes be people in your life who are suspicious of your ability truly to hear God. This is perhaps especially true of direct calling. The very idea of direct calling depends upon a strong affirmation of God's presence and activity in creation. If your driving vision of God is of an absentee creator, you will not make room for the sort of divine speaking and creaturely hearing that are involved in direct calling. Acting obediently to such a vocation requires confidence in the Christian claim that the transcendent God does in fact speak into your life.

Trust is, in fact, a second reason that our portrait of vocation depends on both the immanence and transcendence of God. It is precisely because of both affirmations that you can walk forward in your vocation with complete trust in God. In all three kinds of calling explored in this book, you can see God's immanence reflected in the very act of making God's desires known. A God who infuses each life with a particular role in good and redemptive purposes, as we see in the case of missional calling, is a God who is worthy of trust. By charging us to be signs of the healing of creation, and making that charge knowable to us, God demonstrates concern for the best interests of the whole creation. Furthermore, our trust in God's capacity actually to make good on that redemptive aim depends on our awareness of God's transcendence. Were God part of creation and thus subject to the limitations that mark creaturely life, we really would not have much hope. But our confidence that God transcends those boundaries — of time, of space, of what is possible — yields assurance that God is able to reconcile all creation. When our lives serve as signs of that reconciliation, they point beyond themselves to a God who is both immanent and transcendent.

Our calling to serve as pointers to God's redemptive work leads naturally to a third connection, in this case between vocation and God's transcendence in particular. Acknowledging the mystery involved in God's transcendence yields appropriate humility as you respond to your calling. It is a common temptation to suppose that the results of your efforts must align completely with God's ultimate purposes for creation. If you don't see immediate fruit from working away at your missional calling, for example, you might worry that you are doing something wrong or that your discernment process somehow went awry. But as we saw in Chapter One, there is not an immediate or perfect correspondence between one's efforts and the emergence of the kingdom of God. To suppose that you will be able to recognize all of the ways God might be using your life is to ignore God's transcendence. You simply do not know the complete picture of how God may bring fruit from your response to God's calling. And though it may not initially seem like it, this is good news. It is remarkably freeing not to have the weight of the world on your shoulders. Your job is not to make the kingdom of God a reality on God's behalf; your job is faithfully to live as a sign of God's reconciling work in the way you have been called. Therefore, you can plant seeds, or cultivate ground, or water seedlings with a humble recognition of your dependence on a transcendent God to bring forth the harvest.

The Triune God and Vocation

Along with divine immanence and transcendence, our discussion of vocation has also been shaped by an understanding of

God as Trinity. I fully realize that mentioning the doctrine of the Trinity can bring forth many different reactions from Christians and non-Christians alike. Some people are inclined to scratch their heads at an idea that seems to violate basic mathematics — how can God be both one and three? Others might roll their eyes at the concept, thinking that it might have been useful for past generations but really doesn't seem to "test well" in today's cultural marketplace. Others are happy to ignore the notion altogether, finding it much easier to think about God without any of the seemingly unnecessary window dressing. Despite these attitudes, the doctrine of the Trinity does really matter for us today. As noted in Chapter One, the doctrine of the Trinity makes sense of the biblical portrait of God's saving activity. Think of it this way: the life, death, and resurrection of Jesus are the basis of our reconciliation with God and with each other. The Holy Spirit makes the work of Jesus a reality in our lives now and enables our worship and service of God the Father. This is the sort of activity that is possible only for God, and thus the actions of the Father, the Son, and the Holy Spirit are *all* actions of God. The doctrine of the Trinity reflects the way that the Christian tradition has held this claim together with the conviction that there is only one God: the Father, the Son, and the Holy Spirit are the three persons-in-communion of the one eternal God.

The vision of God as Trinity is essential to our discussion of vocation in two main respects. First, the various ways in which God is involved in your calling and in your response to it can be considered according to the distinct persons of the Trinity. You must be very careful here, however. You should not think of God as a sort of committee, delegating various responsibilities to different members and then reporting back to each other on what happened. The essential unity of the persons of the Trinity means that every act of God in the world is an act of all three persons together. Still, the Christian tradition has been very willing to associate (or "appropriate," to use the technical language) certain actions or characteristics to one or another of the persons of the Trinity. Thus the Father, the Son, and the Holy Spirit are together involved in everything God does in the world, yet it is natural and appropriate to connect a particular action with a particular person of the Trinity in a special way.

How might this work in relation to vocation? Start with the idea that God the Father is ultimately the one who calls. The Father is the person of the Trinity who is associated most directly to the act of creation and to initiating the divine plan of salvation. In that light, it is quite natural to think of the Father as the one who initiates your general, direct, and missional callings. It is true that there are many New Testament narratives in which Jesus, the Son incarnate, offers a direct calling to someone. We might take as examples the calling of Philip (John 1:43), the calling of Levi (Mark 2:13-17), or the remarkable calling of Saul *after* Jesus' ascension (Acts 9:3-6). Still, we must keep in mind Jesus' consistent pattern of describing his work (as Son) as being initiated by the Father. Perhaps the clearest expression of this pattern is in John 6:37-38, where Jesus declares: "Everything that the Father gives me will come to me, and anyone who comes to me I will never drive away; for I have come down from heaven, not to do my own will, but the will of him who sent me." From a biblical perspective, therefore, the Son may extend someone a particular direct calling (in Saul's case, even after Jesus' earthly ministry). But Jesus presented himself as acting on behalf of the Father, whose will shapes the particular ways that Jesus invited and instructed his disciples. Taking the broad view, then, we can appropriate to the Father the act of setting every calling in motion.

This is not to say, of course, that the Son has no crucial role to play in your vocation. On the contrary, the Son's incarnation in the person of Jesus gives a tangible connection to vocation that is indispensable. This is true with respect to general calling, which for Christians is decisively shaped by both the teaching and the example of Jesus. It is true with respect to direct calling, for as we saw in Chapter Two, God's self-revelation in Jesus serves as a crucial criterion for the process of confirming an instance of direct calling. It is also true for missional calling, which we defined in Chapter One as the main contribution one's life makes to God's kingdom. We get the clearest vision of what the kingdom of God looks like in Jesus' life and teaching. Thus the New Testament's witness to Jesus enables you to know the purposes toward which your missional calling is working. The incarnate Son provides the large-scale portrait of God's purposes, and you can thus find where the brushstrokes of your life might fit within it.

You can also recognize distinct roles of the third person of the Trinity, the Holy Spirit, in your vocational life. Specifically, the Spirit makes it possible to recognize your calling and empowers your response. Once again, these roles apply to all three forms of calling. Recall that Scripture is our essential source for recognizing general calling, and the Spirit is most directly associated with our encounter with Scripture. Not only did the Holy Spirit inspire the biblical texts and guide the church in its formation of a New Testament canon, but the Spirit also illuminates our reading of the text in the present. In that respect, the Spirit plays an indispensable role in our knowledge of general calling. This is also true of direct calling. While we noted above that some biblical texts show Jesus as the one who extends the Father's direct calling to someone, it is perhaps more common for the Holy Spirit to mediate a direct calling from the Father. The second half of the book of Acts abounds with examples of this, such as directing the disciples where to go and what to avoid (16:6-7; 20:22-23). We saw throughout Chapter Four how central a role the Holy Spirit plays in the discernment of missional calling as well. By gradually forming you into a person who is able to recognize the intersection of God's purposes and your distinct gifts and passions, the Holy Spirit cultivates the very capacity for discernment. Furthermore, the very ability to follow where God leads you is the result of the Spirit's work in your life.

A second way in which your approach to vocation is shaped by the idea of God as Trinity is your need for relationships. Whether you admit it or not, people were made to live in relationship to each other. Quiet or talkative, shy or outgoing, all people long to know and be known by others. In a very real sense, your identity is deeply shaped by the people who are part of your life. The notion that we are created for community is a direct reflection of our creator. We read in Genesis 1:26 and 1:27 that humanity was created in the image of God. This has often been taken to mean that individual human beings have some capacity that they share only with God — rationality, perhaps, or a moral conscience. That line of thinking can give the impression that we are self-sufficient beings without any need for communion with others. However, when we consider the idea that we are made in the image of a *Triune* God, a very different sort of picture emerges. The one God is, and always has been, three persons-in-communion. At the core of God's being is relationality. To be made in the image of God, then, is to be a relational being. It means that our selfhood is developed and expressed in the context of community. (Stanley J. Grenz develops a fine theological treatment of this idea in *The Social God and the Relational Self*.)

When you get your mind around this understanding of human beings, it becomes immediately clear why community is so central to discerning and living out your vocation. Not only is it the case that you need to involve others in your process of discernment, but you'll also usually find that your missional calling is somehow oriented toward other people. Because people are made in the image of a relational God, the particular purposes to which God calls us will often tend toward healing and deepening relationships. In fact, if a person senses a missional calling that can be lived out as a "lone ranger," it is a good indication that something has gone wrong in the discernment process. We can also see that the confirmation principle that we explored in relation to direct calling is closely connected to our God-given relationality. We are concerned about the costs and consequences of a mistaken claim to direct calling precisely because such claims can destroy relationships in so many ways. The importance of involving wise and mature fellow believers in confirming high-stakes claims to direct calling is apparent, then, when we take seriously our communal nature. Just as God works through others to help you see your calling, you fulfill that calling in the context of a community of faith. As a being created in the image of God, you will find the fullest expression of your humanity in connection with others.

Divine and Human Agency

The recognition that we are created in the image of God leads us to consider how God's activity relates to our activity in fulfilling God's purposes. This question is lurking in essentially every discussion of vocation. The very idea that God calls us to do something or be something suggests that we have a role in God's aims for the world. And yet we have insisted throughout our discussion that the complete fulfillment of God's kingdom depends ultimately on God's action rather than our own efforts. Why should God bother to call us to redemptive activity if God is going to reconcile creation in the end anyway? And if God wishes to involve us in this work, why leave us the freedom to ignore or disobey that calling?

We might begin to address these questions by noticing what creaturely freedom makes possible: the alignment of God's purposes for creation and God's purposes for each of us. A calling is an invitation rather than an act of coercion; room is left for us to respond or not to respond. If we accept the calling, we live into what God wants to do both in us and through us. God could easily have forcefully transformed us into the kind of creatures we were meant to be or — to push it back even further — have programmed us to be obedient from the beginning. But in those scenarios crucial elements of a genuine relationship are missing: freedom, love, and willful interaction. By leaving us space to choose to respond, God has created the possibility of true communion. In that light, living out a calling (in any of the three forms we've discussed) is an act of loving obedience rather than a response to programming. As Eugene H. Peterson writes in his book *Practice Resurrection*, "We hear and respond. We obey. But the obedience is not a trained Pavlovian response to a stock stimulus: 'sit,' 'fetch,' 'roll over.' It takes place in a textured context and personal relationship. It is the act of following a personally addressed command or invitation. We hear our name and respond to the named One who calls us" (p. 34).

True, many biblical narratives would suggest that God takes a stronger hand at times. We have already observed the persistence with which God continues to call Moses in Exodus 3-4, despite Moses' many objections. Jonah's attempt to flee God's calling by heading for Tarshish lands him in the sea (and eventually in the belly of a large fish), leaving us far from surprised when Jonah finally gives in. Saul's blinding encounter with the risen Jesus in Acts 9 would be difficult for even the hardest heart to ignore. Still, there are two things we should keep in mind about such narratives. First, these stories of direct calling, imposing as they are, still required a response. Moses and Jonah in particular may have been reluctant in obedience, but they ultimately chose to do what God had commanded. Second, all three of these characters went on to have further opportunities for obedience and faithfulness. Far from removing the possibility of genuine relationship with God, these vivid examples of direct calling actually drew those characters into the possibility of deeper communion with God.

We should not suppose, of course, that God's activity in the world is restricted to what we do out of obedience. On the contrary, in the midst of our freedom God is at work in ways that we may not know or see. In fact, God is even capable of using our disobedience to accomplish God's purposes. The classical name for God's activity in this regard is divine providence. Affirming God's providence is a way of emphasizing that God is creative enough to work redemptively in a broken world. God is able to use both the good and the bad in the world — including human obedience and disobedience — to bring healing and restoration. God's providential activity is a theme of many biblical texts, and perhaps none are more famous than the Joseph narratives in Genesis. Driven by jealousy, Joseph's brothers had sold him into slavery. They hoped he was out of their lives for good. Yet through a remarkable series of events, Joseph ended up being the means by which God preserved their lives. As they were descendants of Abraham, Joseph was also the means by which God's covenant with Abraham was sustained. When they had reconciled, Joseph said to his brothers: "Even though you intended to do harm to me, God intended it for good, in order to preserve a numerous people, as he is doing today" (Gen. 50:20). In God's boundless creativity, even our worst moments can be turned to redemptive purposes.

We must be extremely careful, however, to keep a clear distinction in mind in any discussion of divine providence. To suggest that God can use our disobedience for redemptive purposes is not at all to suggest that God wants or wills our disobedience. God has given us freedom, and God desires our faithful and obedient response. But if we fail, God is not left at a loss; God can redeem even our bad choices. This is precisely what divine providence means. And as David Bentley Hart contends in *The Doors of the Sea*, such a view is very different from the deterministic view that God somehow *causes* our disobedience. Hart writes,

> It makes a considerable difference, however — nothing less than our understanding of the nature of God is at stake — whether one says that God has eternally willed the history of sin and death, and all that comes to pass therein, as the proper or necessary means of achieving his ends, or whether one says instead that God has willed his good in creatures from eternity and will bring it to pass, despite their rebellion, by so ordering all things toward his goodness that even evil (which he does not cause) becomes an occasion of the operations of grace. And it is only the latter view that can accurately be called a doctrine of 'providence' in the properly theological sense; the former view is mere determinism. (p. 82)

We should not fall into the trap, therefore, of supposing that God "needs" evil or disobedience to accomplish redemptive purposes. On the contrary, God wills good both for us and from us. When we fail to live into that goodness, the idea of providence suggests that God can still work graciously toward God's aims.

Thus we can sum up our reflections on divine and human agency in these terms: God will ultimately and decisively fulfill the purpose of reconciling all creation to God. Until that happens, God is present and active in the world in ways both seen and unseen. The various kinds of calling — general, missional, and direct — are invitations to live as signs of what God is ultimately doing in creation. If we fail to live into those callings, our failure will not thwart God's purposes for the world. Indeed, there is little theological warrant for the common claim that God has no hands or feet in the world other than our own. Yet if we do live into our callings, freely and motivated by love for God, we can move in concert with the movement of God toward the redemption of creation. God neither needs nor compels our participation in building the kingdom; God invites and enables our free and obedient response. The interplay of grace and response draws each of us toward our intended purpose and simultaneously illuminates what God is doing in the world. That convergence is a mark of God's ingenious design.

Living into Vocation as an Act of Worship

One thing is clear in this entire discussion: God is uniquely worthy of being glorified. Worship is the appropriate response to a God who is both immanent and transcendent, who is an eternal communion of love, and who invites our participation in healing the world. When we think of worship, we naturally think of songs, prayers, and the like. These acts of worship are appropriate and essential, and yet we can also think more broadly about worship. One's entire life can be offered as an act of worship. Recall the words of Paul in Romans 12:1-2: "I appeal to you therefore, brothers and sisters, by the mercies of God, to present your bodies as a living sacrifice, holy and acceptable to God, which is your spiritual worship. Do not be conformed to this world, but be transformed by the renewing of your minds, so that you may discern what is the will of God — what is good and acceptable and perfect." Notice the extent of this call to worship — to present our bodies, our whole selves, as a living sacrifice. In responding to God's calling, we worship not just with our voices, but with everything we are.

It would be a mistake to suppose, of course, that this means gathering for intentional worship is unnecessary. The ways in which God has acted in the world for our salvation must be spoken and sung, both to help us remember what God has done and to draw us deeper into that story. As we reflect on God's actions, we come to a deeper sense of who God is — and we proclaim that joyfully in the public reading of Scripture, prayer, songs, confessions, testimonies, and other acts of worship. The Orthodox theologian Alexander Schmemann suggests that even the act of gathering together as a body of believers is an important act of worship and witness. He writes in *For the Life of the World*,

> The journey begins when Christians leave their homes and beds. They leave, indeed, their life in this present and concrete world, and whether they have to drive fifteen miles or walk a few blocks, a sacramental act is already taking place, an act which is the very condition of everything else that is to happen. For they are now on their way to *constitute the Church*, or to be more exact, to be transformed into the Church of God. They have been individuals, some white, some black, some poor, some rich, they have been the "natural" world and a natural community. And now they have been called to "come together in one place," to bring their lives, their very "world" with them and to be more than what they were: a *new* community with a new life. (p. 27, original emphasis)

Schmemann's words are worth reading and rereading, particularly on those Sunday mornings when it seems a bit difficult to get out of bed to go to church. Gathering itself is an act of worship, one that transforms us into a new community with new life. Only by participating in that new life are we prepared to offer the work and the words of the rest of our lives as worship.

And offer it we must. For it would be another sort of mistake to imagine that worship should only take place in the setting of a gathered congregation. By telling and singing God's praises together in gathered worship, we are being equipped to glorify God in our work, our rest, and our interaction with others throughout the entire week. Worshiping the Triune God empowers our mission in the world. Once again it is Schmemann who captures this idea vividly: "It is only as we return from the light and the joy of Christ's presence that we recover the world as a meaningful field of our Christian action, that we see the true reality of the world and thus discover what we must do. Christian mission is always at its beginning. It is today that I am sent back into the world *in joy and peace,* 'having seen the true light,' having partaken of the Holy Spirit, having been a witness of divine Love" (p. 113, original emphasis). Living out our calling, therefore, both is made possible by worship and is itself a means of worship. In this respect, vocation is not only an invitation to action; it is a mode of honoring God.

Schmemann's references to joy, peace, and divine love is a reminder of something crucial. It is not primarily out of a sense of duty or obligation that you should embrace your calling. Responding to God's invitation is a free and joyful act of worship. You express your love for God through your actions in each dimension of vocation. It is true every day as you grow more mature in living out your general calling. It is true as you find new ways to fulfill your missional calling in the changing circumstances of life. It is true as you remain attentive and responsive to any direct calling that God may place on your life. Sometimes as you step forward you have a clear sense of where the road will take you. Sometimes you take the few steps that are known, listening and watching carefully as you go. In all times, propelled by the joy of knowing God, your life can proclaim God's goodness and glory.

DISCUSSION QUESTIONS

1. How has your understanding of God changed over the course of your life?

2. Can you identify times in your life when you clearly sensed God's nearness and presence?

3. Can you identify times in your life when you became deeply aware of God's mystery and otherness?

4. Practically speaking, why is the idea of the Trinity so important to the Christian life?

5. Vocation is about both what God wants to do *through* you and what God wants to do *in* you. What is God doing *in* you at this stage of your life?

Conclusion

People who find their way to books about vocation usually have questions to answer or decisions to make. They hope that what they read might provide a decisive answer, resolve the tension they feel, or ease their frustration. Perhaps these pages have answered some of your questions; perhaps the questions themselves have changed. My hope above all is that you recognize that you can do God's will today, right where you are. That can be difficult to see when you're mired in anxiety about the future or when you're feeling stuck vocationally. But thinking carefully and prayerfully through each of the dimensions of calling can help to clarify the immediate way forward.

Missional calling is what most people have in mind when they think about vocation. The most important thing is not to confuse missional calling with direct calling. A great deal of vocational frustration comes from expecting writing in the sky from God. But as we've seen, not everyone receives a direct calling — and those who do often find that it catches them by surprise. By contrast, everyone has a missional calling to be found through intentional, prayerful discernment. If you don't have a sense for your missional calling, then your way forward is clear: now is the time to begin a process of discernment. If you have identified your missional calling, there is no need to wait for the future to begin living it out. Find ways to fulfill your missional calling in whatever setting you're in. Even when you feel trapped by circumstances, there are always ways to use your gifts and passions to serve as a sign of God's kingdom right where you are.

When it comes to direct calling, there are two kinds of worry that commonly arise. The first is if you are seeking a direct calling that just isn't coming. In such times, it is important to remember that God will get through to you if God has a specific task for you. In the meantime, you can embrace the freedom to find ways to live out your general and missional callings each and every day. The second worry is when you receive a direct calling that you just don't want to hear. Perhaps God is calling you outside of your comfort zone to a task you fear, or perhaps you don't want to be drawn away from what you think is most important. So you may try to ignore or evade that calling. As our exploration of biblical characters has made clear, trying to run from God's calling is nothing new. I'm afraid there are no easy words here — there is no right way forward other than obedience. You might as well respond sooner rather than later.

The primary danger when it comes to general calling is letting it be overshadowed by larger questions about career, marriage, or education. Those questions are important and should be approached with all the thoughtfulness and prayer you can muster. But general calling is the calling that we all share, and it is in front of you each and every day. Do not lose sight of it as you discern missional calling or wrestle with direct calling. Every morning you can wake up and commit to living out your general calling with passion throughout that day. The daily pursuit of God over the long haul adds up to a life that reflects God's kingdom brilliantly. Above all, remember that God is not playing hide-and-seek with you. God's purposes for your life can be known as you grow in knowledge and love of your creator. Seek God with joy and commitment, and your life will unfold beautifully as an act of worship.

Works Cited

Buechner, Frederick. *Now and Then: A Memoir of Vocation*. San Francisco: HarperSanFrancisco, 1983.

————. *The Sacred Journey: A Memoir of Early Days* San Francisco: HarperSanFrancisco, 1982.

Farrington, Debra K. *Hearing with the Heart: A Gentle Guide to Discerning God's Will for Your Life*. San Francisco: Jossey-Bass, 2003.

Foster, Richard J. *Celebration of Discipline: The Path to Spiritual Growth*, 20th Anniversary ed. San Francisco: HarperSanFrancisco, 1998.

Grenz, Stanley J. *The Social God and the Relational Self: A Trinitarian Theology of the Imago Dei*. Louisville, KY: Westminster John Knox, 2001.

Hart, David Bentley. *The Doors of the Sea: Where Was God in the Tsunami?* Grand Rapids: Wm. B. Eerdmans, 2005.

Lewis, C. S. *Mere Christianity* New York: Collier Books, 1952/1960.

McGrath, Alister E. *Theology: The Basics*, 3rd ed. Malden, MA: Wiley-Blackwell, 2012.

Murphy, Roland E. *The Tree of Life: An Exploration of Biblical Wisdom Literature*, 3rd ed. Grand Rapids: Wm. B. Eerdmans, 2002.

Origen. *On First Principles*, G. W. Butterworth, trans. Gloucester, MA: Peter Smith, 1973.

Palmer, Parker J. *Let Your Life Speak: Listening for the Voice of Vocation*. San Francisco: Jossey-Bass, 2000.

Works Cited

Peterson, Eugene H. *Eat This Book: A Conversation in the Art of Spiritual Reading* Grand Rapids: Wm. B. Eerdmans, 2009.

————. *Practice Resurrection: A Conversation on Growing Up in Christ* Grand Rapids: Wm. B. Eerdmans, 2010.

Placher, William C., ed. *Callings: Twenty Centuries of Christian Wisdom on Vocation*. Grand Rapids: Wm. B. Eerdmans, 2005.

Schmemann, Alexander. *For the Life of the World: Sacraments and Orthodoxy* Crestwood, NY: St. Vladimir's Seminary Press, 1973.

Sittser, Jerry. *The Will of God as a Way of Life: How to Make Every Decision with Peace and Confidence*. Grand Rapids: Zondervan, 2004.

Smith, Gordon T. *Courage and Calling: Embracing Your God-Given Potential*. revised and expanded ed. Downers Grove, IL: InterVarsity Press, 2011.

Snyder, Howard A. *Models of the Kingdom*. Nashville, TN: Abingdon Press, 1991.

Taylor, Barbara Brown. *An Altar in the World: A Geography of Faith*. New York: HarperOne, 2009.

Van Duzer, Jeff. *Why Business Matters to God (and What Still Needs to Be Fixed)*. Downers Grove, IL: IVP Academic, 2010.

Ware, Bishop Kallistos. *The Orthodox Way*, rev. ed. Crestwood, NY: St. Vladimir's Seminary Press, 2001.

Wells, Samuel. *Improvisation: The Drama of Christian Ethics*. Grand Rapids: Brazos Press, 2004.

Wesley, John. Sermon 7, "The Way to the Kingdom," I.10. In Albert C. Outler and Richard P. Heitzenrater, eds., *John Wesley's Sermons: An Anthology* Nashville, TN: Abingdon Press, 1991.

————. Sermon 24, "Upon Our Lord's Sermon on the Mount — Discourse IV," I.1. In Outler and Heitzenrater, eds. *John Wesley's Sermons*.

Williams, Rowan. *Tokens of Trust: An Introduction to Christian Belief*. Louisville, KY: Westminster John Knox, 2007.

Wright, N. T. *Simply Christian: Why Christianity Makes Sense*. San Francisco: HarperOne, 2006.

Yamasaki, April. *Sacred Pauses: Spiritual Practices for Personal Renewal.* Harrisonburg, VA: Herald Press, 2013.